VISIT
TO THE
LOGOS OF EARTH

By

GEORGE KING, D.Sc., Th.D.

Published by
THE AETHERIUS SOCIETY
6202 Afton Place, Hollywood, California 90028-8298, U.S.A.

First Published
1986

VISIT TO THE LOGOS OF EARTH

COPYRIGHT OWNED BY
GEORGE KING, D.Sc., Th.D.

VISIT TO THE LOGOS OF EARTH

Published by

THE AETHERIUS SOCIETY

By the same author:

THE NINE FREEDOMS
THE DAY THE GODS CAME
OPERATION SPACE MAGIC — THE COSMIC
    CONNECTION
YOU TOO CAN HEAL
THE TWELVE BLESSINGS
YOU ARE RESPONSIBLE!
THE FIVE TEMPLES OF GOD
THE THREE SAVIOURS ARE HERE!
THE AGE OF AETHERIUS
OPERATION SUNBEAM — GOD'S MAGIC IN ACTION
WISDOM OF THE PLANETS
LIFE ON THE PLANETS
COSMIC VOICE, VOLUME 1
COSMIC VOICE, VOLUME 2
THE FESTIVAL OF "CARRYING THE LIGHT"
DESTRUCTION OF THE TEMPLE OF DEATH
RESCUE IN SPACE
JESUS COMES AGAIN
ETERNAL RECOGNITION OF OPERATION SUNBEAM
SPACE CONTACT IN SANTA BARBARA
MY CONTACT WITH THE GREAT WHITE BROTHERHOOD
BECOME A BUILDER OF THE NEW AGE
THE PRACTICES OF AETHERIUS
CONTACT YOUR HIGHER SELF THROUGH YOGA
BOOK OF SACRED PRAYERS
THE FLYING SAUCERS
THE TRUTH ABOUT DYNAMIC PRAYER
A SERIES OF LESSONS ON CASSETTE IN APPLIED
    METAPHYSICS, ETC.

DEDICATION

This book is respectfully dedicated to the most important, Elevated Beings living on the Planet Earth today, The Three Protectors Of The Ineffable Flame Of The Logos Of Terra.

CONTENTS

ILLUSTRATIONS

 * Illustration painted by John Hamagami.
** Illustration painted by Kalan Brunink.
   Both illustrations executed under the strict supervision of the author.

THE AUTHOR

His Eminence Prince Doctor George King de Santorini, Metropolitan Archbishop of The Aetherius Churches; a Western Master of Yoga who has devoted his life in service to humanity.

INTRODUCTION TO THE AUTHOR

The author of this book was born in the county of Shropshire, England, on January 23rd, 1919. Even from an early age he became interested in religion, at first of an orthodox nature. Later, when he carefully studied what is known today as the metaphysical sciences, he began a diligent practice of certain forms of Yoga. This mystical science was the evolutionary ladder up which he climbed in order to learn about the higher aspects of the multitudinous forms of life which abound on this Planet. Thus, without his realization at that time, he was preparing himself for a major step forward which was due to change the whole of his life and enable him to throw his intensity of purpose and dedication in a direction which would prove to be of great benefit to mankind.

In 1954, out of the blue, came the first Contact, recognizable as such, with Cosmic Intelligences Who lived in other parts of the Solar System. The story of this Contact has been written up by the media, hundreds of times in many different languages. It has been repeated hundreds of times in lectures from the public platforms throughout the United States, England, Nigeria, New Zealand, Australia, Holland and other European countries.

From that initial Contact the author, already capable of bringing about the deep meditative state of Samadhi, was used as a mental channel for over 600 Transmissions given by Intelligences residing on more highly-evolved worlds than this Earth. Some of these Transmissions have been published both in the written word and on cassettes which have circulated throughout many countries and have brought enlightenment and hope to thousands of people.

These Transmissions covered hundreds of different subjects, varying from details of how to put right conditions on the surface of Earth, to deep outer-space science. Some of these Transmissions were also vivid descriptions of mighty battles fought on behalf of mankind by Six Interplanetary Adepts Who live on or close to the surface of Earth. (Note 1.)

Outstanding happenings, such as "The Initiation Of Earth,"

were also vividly described by Cosmic Intelligences, using the author as a mental channel, through whom to give mankind this outstanding and most helpful information. (Note 2.)

In 1955, in answer to a Command delivered by Higher Sources, The Aetherius Society was founded by the author in England and later incorporated in the United States in 1960. Since that time The Aetherius Society has been responsible for the preservation and publication of these great Cosmic Transmissions, all of which are highly elevated teachings of profundity and yet given in a way which can be understood by any thinking researcher.

As well as being made responsible for receiving Cosmic Transmissions, the author was also given many other very important assignments by Cosmic Intelligences; assignments such as "Operation Starlight" and "Operation Bluewater" which, although difficult to perform, were treated by the author as one of the most important aspects of his life. (Note 3.)

After the years of previous self-imposed strict Yoga discipline, he was able to throw the whole of his strength and concentration, sometimes under the most adverse weather conditions, into the performance of the Missions he was asked to undertake by The Cosmic Masters for and on behalf of uncaring mankind. Such assignments are fully described in literature published by The Aetherius Society.

Early in 1966 the author invented and designed a Mission which was to become world-renowned for its importance. This Mission was officially named "Operation Sunbeam" and was accepted into the overall Cosmic Plan for the advancement, enlightenment and salvation of mankind. Although described in detail elsewhere, briefly, "Operation Sunbeam" is a Mission in which Spiritual Energies of the highest frequency are collected and these are radiated, through certain known Psychic Centres of Earth, to The Logos Of Earth as a token Spiritual Energy repayment for what this mighty Cosmic Being has done for all life on this Planet. According to Cosmic Sources — not our idea — "Operation Sunbeam" started a large Spiritual snowball in other parts of this Galaxy.

The author often makes the statement that it was because he

gave his life in unconditional surrender to God that he was so inspired by the God-Force within that he was able to formulate a Mission of such importance as "Operation Sunbeam." (Note 4.)

The author also designed another Mission, called "Operation Prayer Power," which gave Members of the Society an opportunity to send out mass Spiritual Healing to certain disaster areas of the world in a way which had not been done in the past. Powerful energies invoked by Dynamic Prayer were stored in physical containers, to be released when they were necessary as a result of war, famine, disease and earthquake. (Note 5.)

It is interesting to note that certain communist countries of the world have spent vast sums of money in research to be able to store and manipulate psychic energies on a large scale. The author was able to do this many years ago by tapping the all-knowledge space within himself and evolving a new science which has benefited mankind in the past and will continue to do so in the future.

Despite the outstanding feats which the author has been responsible for, he did not at first receive the fame and recognition which he deserved.

Even so, there was a vast and controlled Plan being put into operation by both The Cosmic Masters from other worlds and The Spiritual Hierarchy of Ascended Masters on this Earth. The author had been instructed to hold himself in readiness for an invitation to an assembly arranged by the Highest Powers in The Spiritual Hierarchy in order to extend the range, potency and possibilities of the Mission, "Operation Sunbeam," which he had designed.

At approximately 2:00 p.m. on December 5th, 1978 (Earthyear 15.151), the call came. (Note 6.)

The author, well-versed in certain advanced Yogic techniques, was able to project his consciousness from his physical body and was received with love and understanding by the Members of The Spiritual Hierarchy Of Earth in that mystical floating Temple called "Shamballa," which, for thousands of years, has been the Headquarters through which The Spiritual Hierarchy of this Earth operate. Just like all really Elevated Beings, They respect true protocol in all its forms.

The main reason for the invitation was to ask permission from the designer of "Operation Sunbeam" if They, The Spiritual Hierarchy Of Earth, may advance "Operation Sunbeam" in a way which would not be possible for The Aetherius Society with its limited funding and resources. The author, strictly obeying what may be termed as "mystical protocol," enquired first if these Masters had gained permission from even Higher Authority before the question was posed. Having been assured that the correct protocol had been observed in every minute detail, the author was then put in the singular position of giving his permission to the Ascended Masters for the extension of "Operation Sunbeam" as They proposed, and further, permission to adopt the basic modus operandi which the author had designed through painstaking research.

After this, much to the amazement of the author, he was then approached by the Kumara of Shamballa, Who physically touched him three times; once upon the head, then upon the right shoulder and then upon the left shoulder, and spoke in a physical voice in perfect English, those most significant words:

"I thus Initiate you as 'Grand Knight Templar Of The Inner Sanctum Of The Holy Order Of The Spiritual Hierarchy Of Earth.'"

This mystical Knighthood was bestowed upon the author for his devotion and cooperation with The Cosmic Masters since 1954 and especially for his work in "Operation Sunbeam," which helped to bring about a Karmic stabilization of conditions on the Planet Earth. (Note 7.)

What happens on the Higher Planes is also later manifested on the mento-physical Realms.

Starting early in 1980 (Earthyear 16), the author began to be recognized for his humanitarian work by Orders of Chivalry from different parts of the world. In a short time the author became a highly respected and much-decorated individual as recognition poured in from Princes and Grand Masters of Orders of Chivalry on Earth.

His Royal and Imperial Highness Prince Henri III Paleologue bestowed the title of Count de Florina on Sir George King in the summer of 1980 and he was subsequently Crowned at an official Coronation held in America on May 31st, 1981 (Earthyear

17.328). Previous to this, in 1980, he received from France the much-coveted "l'Etoile de la Paix," only a few of which have ever been given.

Soon after this, on August 23rd, 1980 (Earthyear 17.47), His Excellency Count George King de Florina was anointed, consecrated, appointed and created an Archbishop in the presence of two more Archbishops and a Bishop in America. He was instructed to: "Go forth and found your own religion."

Although The Aetherius Society had been in existence for 25 years prior to this, by ecclesiastical law the release enabled Count George King de Florina to become, His Eminence Metropolitan Archbishop of The Aetherius Churches. This title was soon recognized by other Archbishops from France who bestowed further honours upon His Eminence. Count George King's name also appears in the "1981 Directory of Distinguished Americans" and the Book of European Nobility. His Eminence Count George King was nominated as "Minister of the Year for 1981" by the Board of Directors of the International Evangelism Crusades — a world-wide religious denomination of Ministers in 49 different countries.

Further Knighthoods were bestowed upon Count George King by prominent Orders of Chivalry. He was given high positions in these Orders.

His work for the Republic of Poland (in exile) was also recognized by prominent government officials.

On April 16th, 1981 (Earthyear 17.283), a prominent Cosmic Master — Controller of The Third Satellite and the same Being Who had delivered many outstanding Cosmic Transmissions to Earth, including "The Nine Freedoms" — gave a Transmission unique in the annals of philosophical history on this Planet. (Note 8.)

The main reason for delivering this Transmission through the author was to inform mankind of Cosmic Awards which had been delivered to The Six Adepts for Their untiring devotion to the Cosmic Plan and for what They had done for all life on Earth. (Note 9.) However, towards the end of the Transmission, the following statement, which is a verbatim quotation, was made by the Cosmic Master, Mars Sector 6:

"The Academy Of Space Sciences have made the following Awards of Merit and Honour to George King for the invention and performance of 'Operation Sunbeam':

Saturn Peace Prize for Humanities;

Venus Peace Prize for Humanities;

The Mars Sector 6 Peace Prize for Humanities;

Ruby Medal Of Honour, and two Stars, for Valour;

Rank — classified.''

Again, to repeat for emphasis, what happens on the Higher Planes must, in one way or another, be manifested on the physical Realms.

On July 19th, 1981 (Earthyear 18.12), before a large and distinguished gathering in the Dorchester Hotel, Park Lane, London, His Highness Prince Giuseppe Pensavalle, President of the International Union of Christian Chivalry, gave the much-coveted "Prize of Peace and Justice" to His Eminence in recognition of his tireless work and charity to humanity. This prize, originated by U.N.I.C.E.F., also carries with it the elevated title of "Knight of Humanity." As a further personal compliment, H.H. Prince Pensavalle flew in specially from Rome to give this award. It should be remembered that this Peace Prize is only given very rarely and then only after rigorous enquiries are made by the President and the Grand Council as to the authenticity and deserts of the recipient. The Peace Prize has, in the past, been given to such prominent people as Professor Albert Einstein, Mother Teresa of Calcutta, Dr. Henry Kissinger and Dr. Albert Schweitzer.

On Saturday, September 26th, 1981 (Earthyear 18.81), the Coronation of Their Serene Highnesses Prince George King and Princess Monique King de Santorini was performed by His Royal and Imperial Highness Prince Henri III, Constantin de Vigo Aleramico Lascaris Paleologue at St. George's Church, Hanover Square, London. His Imperial Highness Prince Henri is the legal and recognized Head of the Imperial House of Palaeologus of Byzantium. This Coronation was performed according to the rules of ancient tradition, with the full knowledge and approval of King Umberto of Italy.

In 1981 Prince George was officially appointed as Imperial

Advisor to the Sovereign Imperial and Royal House de Vigo Aleramico Laskaris Palaeologus of Byzantium. He was also given the Grand Collier in the "Imperial Sovereign Military Orthodox Dynastic Constantinian Order of Saint Georges." These appointments brought him onto the Advisory Council of several old and most auspicious Orders of Chivalry.

Soon after being Crowned as His Serene Highness Prince George King de Santorini by H.R. & I.H. Prince Henri III Paleologue, the legal and recognized Head of the Imperial House of Palaeologus of Byzantium, Prince George King founded an Order of Chivalry known as, "The Mystical Order of Saint Peter." H.R. & I.H. Prince Henri Paleologue consented, in deference to Prince George, to become the Eminent Royal Protector of this Order and to extend, through the Prince Grand Master, his "Fons Honorum" (Fountain of Honours) to recipients of Knighthood in the Order, thereby making this Order of Chivalry high among the most legitimate Orders on Earth today.

On September 6th, 1981 (Earthyear 18.61), he was awarded the title of Doctor of Literature and Letters by the North-West London University, which has been established for 66 years. He was given a special Citation for Merit and Excellence for three of his already published books by several Professors, who studied them with very keen interest.

In 1983 his name appeared in "Who's Who in American Law Enforcement," published by the American Police Academy, with full recognition of his title as Prince, for his work as adviser to American law enforcement agencies and the fact that he gave honours to certain distinguished police officers in an Order of Chivalry called the "Royal Knights of Justice," of which he was appointed as Deputy Grand Master. He was later appointed as an International Police Chaplain by the American Federation of Police.

His name has also appeared in the "Golden Book of European Nobility," "Who's Who in California," "Directory of Distinguished Americans," "Famiglie Nobili d'Italia e d'Europe," etc.

He was also appointed to several political Committees and is a Charter Member of the Republican Presidential Task Force, founded by Ronald Reagan, President of the United States.

On July 25th, 1984 (Earthyear 21.18), the North-West London University gave to the author a Doctor of Science degree for his outstanding research thesis in Astro-Metaphysics and the Cosmic Sciences. At the same time, A Citation of Merit was given by the same University for the author's published works, namely, *Operation Space Magic — The Cosmic Connection* and *Operation Sunbeam — God's Magic In Action*. (Note 10.) On June 9th, 1984 (Earthyear 20.337), the International Theological Seminary awarded the author the State approved degree of Doctor of Philosophy in Theology in recognition of his deep study and theses on theological matters. These, together with his other academic qualifications, prove that Prince George King is not only an inspired man of high Spiritual and Religious calling, but is also considered, by those who know, to be capable of rising to the academic heights as well.

On January 3rd, 1983, the author was invited by The Adepts to a certain position where he met The Lord Maitreya, a prominent Ascended Master of The Spiritual Hierarchy Of Earth. On this occasion, The Lord Maitreya, acting as an Emissary of the Supreme Kumara of Shamballa, presented the author with the "Grand Circle" of "The Grand Knights Templar Of The Inner Sanctum Of The Holy Order Of The Spiritual Hierarchy Of Earth." This award is second to the Grand Collier and is only given to the choice few who have performed an outstanding service to mankind and to The Spiritual Hierarchy Themselves. This can be counted as one of the highest honours ever given to anyone in a terrestrial body.

At the same time, the author learned that all of his titles — Prince George King de Santorini, Count de Florina, Metropolitan Archbishop — all degrees and all positions he holds, were recognized by The Spiritual Hierarchy Of Earth forever! This applies for his present life and all of the lives to come, no matter where they may be.

This also validates the titles of H.R. & I.H. Prince Henri III, Constantin de Vigo Aleramico Lascaris Paleologue, as it was under his "Fons Honorum" that the author was Crowned Count de Florina and Prince de Santorini. Although H.R. & I.H. Prince Henri is the legal and recognized Head of the House of Palaeologus of Byzantium, this recognition by The Spiritual Hierarchy Of Earth is the highest possible compliment and recognition of his position.

When an Ascended Master of the calibre of the Supreme Kumara of Shamballa declares you are a Prince, this is recognition forever!

This same recognition applies to his wife, and when they pass on, no matter where they go, be it to another Planet or be it to the Higher Realms of Earth, these titles will always and forever, for eternity, be recognized by The Spiritual Hierarchy of this Earth. (Note 11.)

Thus, in only three years after the initial Ceremony of Knighthood held on Shamballa, H.S.H. Prince George King was given the highest honours which are possible to give to any man who was not born of noble birth.

Indeed there was a Master Plan at work which inspired The Cosmic Masters as well as people in position on Earth, to recognize the untiring work for mankind of an individual and to come forward most boldly with this recognition.

These are some of the many high honours which were bestowed upon the Founder–President of The Aetherius Society by great people who had come to recognize His Eminence for what he was — a man completely dedicated to God and to the salvation of humanity.

Years before this, he had been recognized, carefully analyzed and later chosen by Cosmic Forces as, ''Primary Terrestrial Mental Channel,'' and it is in this capacity that he writes this book, *Visit To The Logos Of Earth.*

AUTHOR'S RECOMMENDATIONS

NOTE 1. For information on the horrendous battles fought by The Mighty Six Adepts for the protection of all life on Earth, read *The Three Saviours Are Here!* This unique book gives the account of actions of vital importance to the salvation and future evolution of mankind and contains information unobtainable from any other source. Also read *Destruction Of The Temple Of Death/Rescue In Space* and *The Atomic Mission*.

NOTE 2. On July 8th, 1964, The Cosmic Masters, Who comprise The Spiritual Hierarchy of the Solar System, performed the most advanced Astro-metaphysical Operation which had ever been reported to mankind — The Primary Initiation Of Earth. Under the guiding genius of a highly-evolved Cosmic Being, streams of Divine Initiating Energies were directed into the very Heart of the living, breathing Goddess — Earth. The author was privileged to be the only channel through whom the report of this stupendous event was given to mankind, and this was subsequently published in his unique book, *The Day The Gods Came*.

NOTE 3. Between July 1958 and August 1961, in cooperation with Higher Cosmic Forces, Doctor George King undertook an arduous metaphysical Operation, "Operation Starlight," in which 19 Holy Mountains were Charged with Spiritual Energies, to be used by ordinary man. Read the pamphlet, *The Holy Mountains Of The World*, and listen to Cassette No. C-27, *Deep Occult Revelations About Operation Starlight*.

"Operation Bluewater" was a complex metaphysical Operation performed in 1963 and 1964 off the coast of California, U.S.A., the success of which prevented a major earthquake and resultant tidal wave which would have devastated a large part of the western American coastline. The Operation, assigned to the author by Cosmic Forces, involved the transmission of immense Spiritual Energies to the Planet Herself as an Entity, and was an essential task prior to "The Initiation Of Earth."

For details of this Cosmic Mission, read the booklet, *This Is The Hour Of Truth*, and *The Aetherius Society Newsletter*, Volumes 2, 3 and 4, 1963–1965.

NOTE 4. The Cosmic Mission, "Operation Sunbeam," has been declared by Higher Forces to be the most important action being performed on Earth today, being unequalled in its Karmic power to benefit all life on Earth. Further understanding of this Mission can be gained by a study of the following Aetherius Society publications:

Cassette No. C-54, *Operation Sunbeam;* Metacassette® No. MC-2, *Operation Sunbeam Inspires The Galaxy* — a Transmission from a Cosmic Master explaining the immense ramifications of the Mission; and Metacassette® No. MC-19, *Gotha Speaks To Earth* — a Transmission describing the reason for the presence on Earth of advanced Intelligences from the System of "Gotha" in order to help in the Cosmic Mission, "Operation Sunbeam."

The booklet, *Operation Sunbeam — God's Magic In Action,* reveals some of the astounding Karmic repercussions of "Operation Sunbeam," and contains a report of a meeting, attended by Doctor George King as the designer of the Mission, at which his permission was given to The Spiritual Hierarchy Of Earth to perform "Operation Sunbeam."

The history of this Mission has also been recorded in *The Aetherius Society Newsletter* and Journal, *Cosmic Voice.* Details are obtainable from the publishers, The Aetherius Society.

NOTE 5. "Operation Prayer Power," a Cosmic Mission designed by the author, is the most potent mass healing tool ever devised for the use and benefit of ordinary man. For a greater understanding of this vital Mission, study of the following cassettes is recommended:

Cassette No. C-52, *Operation Prayer Power;* Metacassette® No. MC-12, *Operation Prayer Power — A Spiritual Dream Come True;* Metacassette® No. MC-13, *Important Declaration Of Truth To Terra.* Also listen to Metacassette® No. MC-21, *The Inauguration Of Operation Prayer Power On Level Four,* for an account of the extension of this vitally important Mission to the subtle Realms of Earth.

The history of this Mission is also recorded in *The Aetherius Society Newsletter* and Journal, *Cosmic Voice.* Details are available from the publishers.

For information on how to participate in this on-going Mission, contact your nearest Headquarters of The Aetherius Society and read the pamphlet, *Operation Prayer Power — A Spiritual Dream Come True*, obtainable free of charge.

NOTE 6. In recognition of The Primary Initiation of the Planet Earth on July 8th, 1964, an event described in full in the author's book, *The Day The Gods Came*, the Higher Realms altered Their calendars and regarded July 8th, 1964 as Earthyear 1, Earthday 1, and continued from there.

NOTE 7. Read *Operation Sunbeam — God's Magic In Action* for full details of one of the major results brought about by the performance of "Operation Sunbeam," and a description of the mystical Knighthood bestowed upon the author.

It should be made clear that "The Grand Knights Templar Of The Inner Sanctum Of The Holy Order Of The Spiritual Hierarchy Of Earth" is not connected to any Order of Chivalry existing on the physical planes of Earth. This mystical Order was founded thousands of years before Chivalry was known on this Earth, and undoubtedly acted as an inspiration for the Chivalric movement as a whole.

NOTE 8. Study of the profound Teachings delivered by the Cosmic Master, Mars Sector 6 is highly recommended to all New Age students.

See the following books: *The Nine Freedoms; The Day The Gods Came; You Are Responsible!; Wisdom Of The Planets; Life On The Planets; Cosmic Voice, Volume 1; Cosmic Voice,* Issues 22 through 26; *Join Your Ship; A Cosmic Message Of Divine Opportunity.*

The following Metacassettes® contain Transmissions from this Cosmic Master, recorded as they were delivered: MC-9, *Power Transmissions For Members;* MC-10, *Watcher In The Night;* MC-12, *Operation Prayer Power — A Spiritual Dream Come True;* MC-14, *Ye Are Gods;* MC-15, *From Freewill To Freedom;* MC-16, *Action Is Essential;* MC-17, *Fight Ye The Evil;* MC-18, *Be Sane Ye Men.*

NOTE 9. The full text of this very significant Transmission, together with explanation by the author, is contained in *Cosmic Voice,* Volume 2, Issues 7 & 8, May 1981.

NOTE 10. The five books which were given a special Citation by the North-West London University, with their names mentioned on the official documents, were, *The Day The Gods Came*, *The Nine Freedoms*, *You Too Can Heal*, *Operation Space Magic — The Cosmic Connection* and *Operation Sunbeam — God's Magic In Action*.

NOTE 11. See *Eternal Recognition Of Operation Sunbeam*, published by The Aetherius Society.

All cassettes, books and Newsletters recommended above are currently available from the publishers, The Aetherius Society.

ALL MATERIAL MANIFESTATION IS A RESULT OF THE APPLICATION OF DIVINE MIND WHICH CREATED MULTITUDINOUS ENERGY FIELDS IN WHICH PARTICLES OF MATTER ARE HELD IN CONTINUOUS MOTION.

THERE IS ONLY ONE ENERGY CRISIS IN THE WORLD TODAY — THAT IS, THE SPIRITUAL ENERGY CRISIS. IF THIS IS PUT RIGHT WITHIN THE HEARTS AND MINDS OF MANKIND, THEN NO OTHER MAN-MADE SHORTAGES CAN EXIST.

CHAPTER 1

EVOLUTION OF A MISSION

Despite the fact that man is dependent upon the combination of elements provided by the Earth for the sustenance of the body in which he lives, very little is known about its construction. Although man has landed his kind on the moon and sent probing satellites throughout different parts of the Solar System into outer space, little has been learned about inner space. Scientists are still advancing theories as to the construction of this Planet which, for the most part, have been formulated from observations of the outer crust. Officially, science has, as yet, not penetrated the terrestrial crust very much deeper than about 10 miles. This is a short distance when you realize that the diameter, through the Earth from North to South Pole, is approximately 8,000 miles.

Man has learned that, in certain places, the deeper he goes into the Earth's crust the warmer it becomes. The temperature increases approximately 20° centigrade per kilometer. Some scientists say that the inner core of Earth has temperatures of between 2,000°–3,000° centigrade. Some believe that the Earth is solid all the way through, with an inner core made of radioactive rock which, at the centre, exerts pressures of up to 21,000 tons per square inch. They view the Earth then, as more or less a solid mass, made up from different layers of rock and magma. In the view of orthodox science the magma layer, although only vaguely referred to, is a layer of heavy molten material and they are not even sure of what this material is made. Science speculates that lava issued from volcanoes at 2,000° centigrade or more, is pushed up by internal pressures and may be parts of the boiling magma.

Despite the fact that the Planet is regarded by some as a solid dense mass, science has proved that there is continual movement on the surface. In some parts of the world, large rock formations have been seen to move several miles in just a few years. Some scientists even state that this creeping in the outer crust of the Planet caused the continents to break away from each other, thereby causing a division of land masses. From a metaphysical point of view, the Earth, while having some of the characteristics described by science, is vastly more complex than scientists have yet discovered.

It is a proven fact that what the metaphysician says today is verified by the scientist tomorrow.

I have made statements about the movement and increase of certain natural phenomena, many of which have now been proven and thereby accepted by science. Similar occurrences have happened continually throughout the ages.

There is nothing haphazard in Creation.

All aspects of Creation dovetail together into one perfect interrelated whole. And each part of the whole is created in such a fashion as to perform a very definite function. A terrestrial human body, as we know it, can survive on this Planet but the same terrestrial body, without artificial environment, could not survive for long on one of our nearest neighbours in the Solar System, such as Mercury. Yet we have been informed throughout the past 25 years that Mercury, like the Planet Earth, is inhabited. This information was not the result of scientific expostulation but came directly from outer space Travellers Who, in Their lifetimes, had actually visited the Planet Mercury; in other words, could give us first-hand information through experience — not just an educated guess. The atmosphere surrounding Earth is quite different from the atmosphere surrounding Venus, for instance, and yet again, we have been told that Venus is also inhabited by Life Forms Who, while living in a physical body like we on Earth do, have a different mineral based cellular structure. (Note 1.)

The more one delves into research, whether that research is of inner space or outer space, the more one discovers the perfection of the initial Creation.

As with the body of a Planet, so it is on a smaller scale with the body of a human. This, too, is far more versatile than science has admitted to date. As this book is written for the more advanced occult student, it is not my intention, at this stage, to prove the validity of capabilities such as extrasensory perception, mental telepathy and astral projection. I will assume that the reader is familiar with these capabilities. If not, many writers, highly specialized in their individual fields, have laid the case for the existence of this type of advanced phenomena before the public. Suffice it is for me to say that, with the use of meditation in its deepest occult sense, mental telepathy and certainly astral projection, one can travel freely and gain Wisdom and knowledge as a result of such travel, unhampered by the limitations of the delicate human frame.

It is through the employment of such faculties that the advanced metaphysician is able to learn more and learn quicker than his orthodox brother who feels he must put his discoveries into a scientific formula before they are acceptable. That is why the occult scientist, or as I call him, the meta-scientist, is, in many cases, hundreds of years ahead of orthodoxy and let us bear in mind that, such a meta-scientist, if correctly trained either in this life or the last, can gain information which is, if anything, more valid than that of his orthodox counterpart.

132,000 years ago, the Egyptian priests knew as much about the movement of the Planets in this Solar System as we know today. In fact, they knew more about the importance of these Planets than science will learn for a long time to come. It is not by chance that the Egyptian astronomers and astrologers all agreed that the most important body in our Solar System, apart from the Sun, was the Planet Saturn, even though it was not the largest. This information has been verified from practical experiences which the writer has enjoyed within the last quarter century. (Note 2.) Again, an illustration of the application of the higher forces within man gaining information years ahead of the mathematician.

When some people, myself included, started to study in earnest, by applying what may be termed as extrasensory powers, we became very concerned about man's pollution of the Planetary surface. I am one of the many who, because of this concern, started what is known today as the "ecological movement." We admit that those people interested in promoting ecological balance today, for the most part, are not going far enough, neither are they concentrating on the most important aspects of ecology. However, there are a few who are, with the idea of helping to bring back that original perfect balance to the Planet upon which we completely depend.

It is this motive which caused me to formulate a Mission which is called, ''Operation Earth Light.'' This was not the only reason the Mission was designed; there was another reason which, in my estimation, was far more important than my own discoveries. Some explanation of this must now be given.

This Planet is a living, breathing Entity. It is an ancient and, in comparison with man, very advanced Entity. It is a female Entity. The mass of liquid which covers most of the surface of this Planet and which, in deep occult circles, represents psychic power, illustrates that the Life Stream, or Logos, of this Planet is female in character. Unlike certain other Planets in this Solar System, Earth is very temperate in environmental conditions and is continually promoting the growth of vegetation, animals and human bodies alike. Another striking indication of Her female characteristics. Some Planets, male in character, are, from a temperature point of view, not nearly as temperate, neither is Their surface covered by vast stretches of water and vegetation. Even though such Planets are habitable, They can only be inhabited by entities advanced enough to live under such conditions. Another definite indication of the female characteristics of our Logos — continual promotion and propagation of life in multitudinous forms from Her body is perpetually taking place. We are told that because of the extreme fertility of Earth, it is, in many respects, the most pleasant Planet upon which to live.

If man were to regard himself in the correct manner he would see that he was an essence of the Divine, and that essence had clothed itself in a workable but nevertheless robot-like machine, driven by mind and electrical impulses, in order to gain experience. That this Divine Spark had formulated what, for want of a better word, may be termed, the soul. Beneath this, it had also formulated sensory abilities controlled by the superconscious, conscious and subconscious mind levels so that it could, not only gain experience, but understand this experience. That this Divine Spark had existed ever since Creation began and that it moved with its mental counterparts through experience cycle after experience cycle — through life after life — gaining further experience and conscious control over matter as this long journey was made.

I maintain there is no logic ever propounded which is above this or which can ever prove it wrong. Ancient Beings Who, thousands of years ago had conquered space, have made and verified those statements. Therefore, man, regarding himself in this fashion, would immediately see that his continual lives on this Planet Earth were similar to times in the life of a student visiting the numerous classes in a university. Man would see that he was indeed a student attending the university called Earth, studying a course called, experience and control of matter.

Furthermore, a man who had gained this knowledge of his true being would then appreciate, to a far greater extent than those who had not gained this perception, his dependence, not only upon the Divine Spark itself, but also upon the Planet which gives to him the opportunity to live through his experience cycles. The more these thoughts were uppermost in his mind, the greater love and appreciation he would have to show to, not only the physical body of the Earth, but also its very Life Force. As well as this, the enlightened man would appreciate, far more than the ignorant man, the depth of his indebtedness to the Earth as an Entity for forming that environment which was necessary to aid his present experience cycle.

Such concepts as these made it very obvious to me that it was necessary for someone on this Planet to formulate a procedure which enabled some token form of repayment to be made to the Life Form of the Planet. Having had previous experience in the little-known science of astro-metaphysics — which is the collection and radiation of subtle frequencies of energy to a given destination for a predetermined reason — I formulated a Mission which I called ''Operation Sunbeam.'' This has been thoroughly written up in Aetherius Society literature. (Note 3.) But to reiterate very briefly, ''Operation Sunbeam'' consisted of four major parts:

1. Discovery and knowledge of Psychic Centres of Earth.
2. Making equipment to contain and control subtle energies.
3. Invoking the subtle energies.
4. Transmitting those subtle energies through Psychic Centres which were receptive and able to absorb them, into the inner nervous system of Earth.

I started by inventing a Spiritual Energy battery which was capable of containing Spiritual Energy of ultra-high frequencies. It is one thing to charge such a battery but another thing entirely to be able to discharge it at will. By applying the natural laws, put here in the beginning by the Creator, I was able to devise a simple but effective apparatus which would discharge the Spiritual Energy contained in the carefully prepared crystal contents of this battery at any given time. As far as the invocation of Spiritual Energies was concerned, because of a happening some years ago, there was intervention made on the part of some Masters from another Solar System in our Galaxy Who learned about my research and experimentation. Because these Highly Elevated Beings wished to help in what, to Them, was a truly worthy cause, They were able to offer Their help by agreeing to invoke all the Spiritual Energy necessary for the successful performance of ''Operation Sunbeam.'' (Note 4.)

In the meantime, through personal contact with Higher Beings and the employment of the deeper states of meditation, I was able to discover the whereabouts of certain Psychic Centres of this Earth which would be receptive to such Spiritual Energies. Having gained permission from Higher Authority in the correct way, which I will deal with later in this book, I was then able to start ''Operation Sunbeam'' on September 24th, 1966 (Earthyear 3.79). The Spiritual Energy contained in the first two batteries was placed directly into a Psychic Centre of Earth and from there, it being a female, or receptive, Psychic Centre, this ultra-high frequency of energy was taken down through the nadic, or subtle nervous system of the Earth as an Entity and used directly by The Logos of this Planet.

The gigantic and apparently hopeless task of making some repayment to The Logos for what She had given to all of us throughout our lives here — had begun! Even though at first in ''Operation Sunbeam'' the process was a slow one, however, it was better than nothing at all.

More than once, in a deeper state of much sought after Cosmic Consciousness, I had become vitally aware of what mankind owed to the Earth and intended to at least start a system of repayment. (Note 5.)

If this were a fiction story it would be rejected on the grounds of its improbability, not because of the scientific manipulation of psychic energy, but because every man and woman on Earth capable of sentient thought did not come forward to offer their help and backing to what obviously was the greatest ecological tool ever devised and used for their own benefit.

In the beginning I recognized "'Operation Sunbeam'' as an ecological tool which would gradually, but nonetheless surely, start to manipulate the heavy negative Karma which the masses had brought onto their shoulders by their unappreciative and thoughtless rape of a green, beautiful and Holy Planet. Through life after life the masses had been born and reborn on this Earth — which should have been regarded as a living Temple of the living God — and yet how seldom throughout those centuries have even the few thanked their God and The Logos Of Earth for providing such a beautiful classroom in which to learn their evolutionary lessons. In my humble estimation, such a happening is unbelievable but, I regret to say, very true. If you want a demonstration of gross ignorance on the part of the inhabitants of a magnificent world, then this surely must be an horrific illustration of this. And what is, too, almost unbelievable but unfortunately true, is the fact that, although "'Operation Sunbeam,'' in the beginning anyway, received some publicity through the media, the Mission was performed and financed by a relative handful of people — when millions should have pleaded for the opportunity to help in every way possible to them! It is this part of the Truth which must surely be classed as unbelievable.

However, man, in his ignorant lack of awareness, was not cognizant of the fact that he was being carefully watched by Visitors from Space Who had observed him for many centuries. Only the few had such awareness. Since 1955, I have been given what I consider to be the undeserved honour and privilege of being the human channel through whom over 600 Transmissions of a highly elevating, educational nature were given to Earth by Cosmic Beings. One of these great Cosmic Masters, known as The Master Aetherius, stated on December 18th, 1966 (Earthyear 3.164), that:

"'Operation Sunbeam' has triggered off a line of thought which has its repercussions from one end of this Galaxy to another. Many inhabited worlds in this Galaxy have, in the past, made a token energy gift to The Logos which supports them, but many have not. The inhabitants of Earth are a very backward race, extremely primitive, and yet, in the midst of such savagery as that displayed by terrestrial man throughout his bloody history, has come an offer to give back to the supporting Logos an energy token in honour and regard for Her Divine patience.

"Believe me, ladies and gentlemen, this has triggered off a thought — even an ambition — throughout this Galaxy. Races which, up to this date, had looked up to more advanced individuals than themselves in such a way that they felt that they were not worthy of making a sacrifice to their supporting Logos have, now that this has been done upon Terra, changed their whole concept.

"Even as I speak now to you, literally hundreds of worlds' inhabitants, who before thought themselves totally inadequate, are now preparing, in their different ways, an Operation similar to that you know as 'Operation Sunbeam.'

"In fact, I would go so far as to say that here, upon Terra, in the mind of one individual, was built a sphere which is liable to become one of the largest snowballs in the whole of Galactic history."

Where terrestrials had failed — non-terrestrials succeeded!

So it was that a concept born in the mind of a man living in an ordinary body on the Planet Earth, snowballed into gigantic proportions. This history is written in the Akashic Records of Earth for all those who are advanced enough to read for themselves and because of this, stands as an undeniable Truth in the annals of progress.

The same Cosmic Master Who informed us about this Operation being accepted and performed by more backward worlds than that He came from, also stated that "Operation Sunbeam" was, because it was a beneficial Karmic manipulation for all men, the most important Mission being undertaken on Earth today by terrestrials.

It is easy, in the light of such honours given to an individual, for that person to become complacent, like a soldier becoming content because he has won his first medal. But the nearer that individual can approach the Divine Spark within, the more he becomes aware of the need of suffering humanity. Some have, in the past, devoted their lives to medical study without thought of reward. A very few have even gone to areas afflicted by disease, such as the tropics and leper colonies, in order to administer to the suffering masses there. Others have, as missionaries, helped to spread the word of Christianity and other Religions into the dark ignorant parts of the world. Others have fed the starving millions. Others, probably the fewest of all, have come right down to the heart of man's problems by helping to relieve some of the Karmic pressures which he has brought to bear upon himself. Those who helped in "Operation Sunbeam" belong to these elite few. The repercussions of "Operation Sunbeam" on the Karmic pattern of mankind were absolutely enormous. These are written up elsewhere in our literature. (Note 6.)

Getting back to the rejection of complacency, even though the Operation was gradually bringing about the results which were predetermined in the beginning, I nevertheless was not fully satisfied with its progress and began to investigate other methods of performing this great Spiritual Mission — performed purely as a public service to mankind, by the way, without any financial gain either to myself or to The Aetherius Society. In 1977 (Earthyear 14), I instituted a carefully thought out research programme — which had to be specially designed because of the limitation of funds available for it. After research in the field and very careful study of the action and reaction of the Psychic Centres which I had discovered, I was able to, not only speed up the discharge of Spiritual Energy to the Earth through these Psychic Centres, but also design a modus operandi which enabled the Three Masters Who were invoking the Spiritual Energy on our behalf, to greatly potentize Their output and thus, for the first time in the history of "Operation Sunbeam," on June 14th, 1979 (Earthyear 15.342), was able to direct a stream of Spiritual Energy, unerringly across hundreds of miles, into a Psychic Centre where I knew by previous in-the-field testing, it would be accepted and absorbed by the wonderful Logos of this great Planet. Not only that, but in the course of only two hours, the Masters were able to send an amazing 3,000 Prayer Hour equivalent of Spiritual Energy directly into this Psychic Centre! This Spiritual Energy was invoked by

The Cosmic Masters, from Mount Adams in the Presidential Mountain Range, U.S.A., and sent through our newly designed apparatus which was tuned in to a chosen Psychic Centre of the Mother Earth.

A Prayer Hour is the amount of Spiritual Energy which can be invoked by Dynamic Prayer recited with all one's love and feeling in one hour, non-stop. The quality and quantity vary in certain cases, but as far as The Cosmic Masters are concerned, the quality and quantity of Spiritual Energy invoked by Them can be guaranteed to be of a much higher vibration, or frequency, than that which can be invoked by any terrestrials.

Previous to this, using the older system, our batteries would only hold the equivalent of 1,500 Prayer Hours of Spiritual Energy per battery. It took us 10 years of hard work to discharge 21 such batteries, totaling the approximate equivalent of 31,000 Prayer Hours. With the new system, which I evolved, it took only 48 hours 55 minutes to discharge 63,000 Prayer Hours of Spiritual Energy. For those people who, through lack of experience, are unable to realize what 63,000 hours represents, the following information will be useful to help your comprehension of this:

63,000 Prayer Hours equals: 7 years, 2 months, 9 days and 4 hours.

The average person works 40 hours per week and has 2 weeks holiday per year; therefore, he works for 50 weeks at 40 hours per week in a given year, so that his working year is 2,000 working hours.

Providing a person was capable of invoking this amount of Spiritual Energy non-stop, it would take him a total of 31½ working years to invoke the same amount of Spiritual Energy as that used to accomplish these 21 Phases.

31½ working years equals: 7,875 working days. (Note 7.)

A vast potentization of ''Operation Sunbeam'' had been brought about.

In only 48 hours and 55 minutes, spread out over the period between June 14th and October 28th, 1979, Spiritual Energies which previously would have taken us years to manipulate were given back to The Logos Of Earth.

And that was just the beginning.

Because "Operation Sunbeam" is an on-going Mission, since October 28th, 1979 (Earthyear 16.113), we have been able to manipulate a further 456,000 Prayer Hours of high frequency Spiritual Energies to The Logos Of Earth through two Psychic Centres thousands of miles apart.

At long last a few terrestrials, believing that their faith in God had to be demonstrated by true Service to mankind, and under the leadership of their Spiritual Master, were making a repayment on behalf of the whole human race to that Being to Whom everyone owes so much — the magnificent Logos Of Earth. Because of the sacrifice and effort expended by all of us in The Aetherius Society towards the vitally important project called "Operation Sunbeam," we exerted those manipulative pressures on the Karmic Law which allowed Three Cosmic Masters to help, which They did, by invoking the Spiritual Energies necessary, thus ensuring the success of this world-evolving Mission.

THE INITIATION OF THE SOLAR SYSTEM

Now, to retrace our steps and go back in time to July 8th, 1964.

This is the most important day in the history of mankind on Earth!

On July 8th, 1964 (Earthyear 1.1), The Logos of the Planet Earth was given a stupendous Spiritual Energy Initiation by Cosmic Beings. I wrote a book giving the full information and explanation of this greatest event in the history of mankind called, *The Day The Gods Came*, and this was published by The Aetherius Society. (Note 8.)

During this Initiation vast energies were sent directly to The Logos Of Earth.

Now, She had one of two choices to make:

1. Use these energies immediately.
2. Retain these energies for gradual use throughout the future.

The fact that there are 4½ billion people still living in physical bodies on the Planet Earth proves, beyond any doubt, that She, The Logos Of Terra, chose to keep these energies within Her majestic Heart and not release them immediately. You do not have to be an advanced metaphysician, surely, to realize what would have happened had She released this stupendous energy charge all at once. The vibration of every molecule and atom which makes up the body of this Planet would have been accelerated to such an extent that life on Earth, as we now know it, would not be possible. That only the few who were advanced enough to be capable of living within this vibratory framework could possibly have existed. Bear in mind, I am not only referring to the physical Realms as most of you know them, but also to six of the seven Realms of life above the physical Realm of this Earth, and those of the "hells" beneath this physical Realm. (Note 9.) The vast majority of terrestrials would have had no other course of action but to find another Planet upon which to gain experience. I fully realize this is one of the most far-reaching statements ever made in the history of philosophy but I stand by it to the letter for, not only have I received this Revelation in my deepest meditation, but also this deep Revelation has been confirmed by Beings Who are thousands of years ahead of us in every way.

A somewhat similar happening occurred throughout the Solar System when, apart from Earth, the Planets received an Initiation, the report of which was given on December 28th, 1969 (Earthyear 6.174). During this stupendous event, which was not described in detail to us but just reported by the Cosmic Master Aetherius, unimaginably vast quantities of Spiritual Energies, vibrating in an extremely high frequency framework, were sent to all of the other Planets in this Solar System.

But there was no comparison between the reaction on these more advanced worlds when compared with the reaction on Earth.

We were informed that almost all Life Forms, from the highest to the lowest, were ready to absorb some of these vibrant Spiritual Energies and as a result, these Life Forms were lifted onto a different level of existence! According to information, this unparalleled advancement, enjoyed by the advanced Life Forms, did not in any way impair Their normal functions, but rather advanced the Beings so that Their experience cycles through Evolution could be more deeply appreciated by the individual and collective Life Forms.

In order to do justice to this stupendous Cosmic Event, we are publishing, in full, the Transmission as it was delivered by The Master Aetherius. Like all great Masters, Who really know Their subject very well, The Master Aetherius delivered this Transmission in simple terms which were not only in beautifully phrased prose but easily understandable to we mere mortals.

THE MASTER AETHERIUS

"Good afternoon.

"This afternoon I will deal very briefly with the Initiation of our Solar System.

"The Initiation of all Life Forms on the major Planets of this Solar System, with the exception of Terra, has now been completed. This vast and difficult Cosmic movement was gradually put into operation over the past few of your months. But, of course, a movement on this scale cannot be spoken of in a measured time sequence, as you on Terra know time.

"The Great Lords have planned this for many centuries and had to make it with, as you no doubt can appreciate, great care and only after giving full attention to major details.

"Contrary to appearances, the Initiation of Terra went as expected; the results were exactly as predicted. After this came the stupendous struggle with alien forces, later to be followed by 'Operation Karmalight.' Each Mission was performed in the correct Karmic manner. (Note 10.)

"While this was proceeding, the Initiation of the major part of this System was being put into operation and, at what you would call the right time, the Cosmic movement was made. As a result of this, all Life Forms, except the most involved, were vibrated onto a different physical level of existence. All intelligent Life Forms were not only vibrated onto a higher physical plane of existence, but They have since been able to take with Them essential equipment necessary for Their further Evolution. Even the most advanced animal and vegetable forms have now been lifted to a higher frequency of vibration. As a result of this, we can now operate to a more complete extent than we could before this Cosmic Initiation.

"As you know, Life Forms on Planets like Mars, Venus, Jupiter and similar Planets, were able to change from one physical level of existence to another one at will. But often the energy necessary to remain at this higher level of vibratory existence was considerable. Now we have more complete mastery and control over all aspects of being without the expenditure of vast amounts of energy. This gift to us will make each one of us more productive and will enable each and every one of us to put together the pattern of evolutionary progression in a less limited manner.

"Indeed does the Divine Architect of Creation work in mysterious ways Its Wonders to perform.

"Although Terra was screened from the Initiatory Energies, however, all life forms upon this Planet will benefit in many ways through our progression. One outstanding benefit which you will enjoy — when you have earned it — will be that when you progress from Terra to a higher Planet, you, too, will have the ability to live in this higher vibratory state to which I have referred.

"Another benefit which you upon Terra will reap from the Cosmic movement will be that now the Planets are open to your exploration.

"No longer need they be closed to you as they were up until this time, for even when you visit these, and now you will, sooner or later, you, by such visits, will only learn those secrets you have earned. Previous to this Initiation we could not allow any of you to land your machines on any other inhabited world because we would have had to screen our activities from you. Now the Gods have done this most effectively.

"You can walk the surface of Mars for a thousand of your years without making any discovery which you have no right to make.

"You can now live on some Planets for ten thousand of your years and, until you are ready, you could still erroneously conclude that they were not inhabited, save by basic vegetation forms.

"Just as some dwellers from other parts of this Galaxy could come onto Terra and be unaware of the presence of terrestrial man, so you, too, can visit other Planets without being aware of intelligent life unless that intelligence sees fit to make its presence known.

"Your explorers have already spoken to you with forked tongues regarding their findings upon the simple moon which is your neighbour. Already information gathered during the landings upon Luna has been carefully screened and you have been told what authority saw fit to tell you — no more. This type of situation will continue, but rest assured that there must come a time, because of your evolutionary position, that a great change will take place in this respect.

"It is not part of the Divine Law to keep life forms in confinement, even in Planetary confinement; neither is it in the Divine Law to keep life forms in ignorance.

"As you move out towards the other worlds, so also will your internal systems change, until you will be just as informed of conditions and discoveries as those who experience them. This is so.

"This change, brought about by the evolution of Life Forms on the major Planets in the Solar System, does not invalidate your teachings, although now the brief picture given of life on the Planets must, in the light of these Revelations, be brought up to date.

"The Planets Themselves as Entities, accepted only a fractional amount of the initial power offered to Them. They decided to hold Their Initiation in abeyance and The Lords agreed, so that They could continue existence in Their present state. By so doing, They could remain of Service to evolving Life Forms in other parts of this Galaxy and evolving, in certain ways, terrestrial man. The concept behind this decision, arrived at by The Logoi of these Planets, would be too deep to express in your language. Suffice to say that They made the decision referred to for some of the reasons given.

"And thus it has been done.

"Now Life Forms Who have enjoyed the fruits of Their evolution by this great happening can be of even greater Service than They were before and indeed, have already started to spread Themselves through the Galaxy. Yes, and will go even beyond these confines at a date in the not too far distant future. Demonstrating, by action, They will go, touching with Their minds those other life forms ready for such contact. And thus, slowly, surely, another aspect of the great Plan for the total Evolution of all beings will be worked out in perfection, which is the Governing Law behind it all.

"And you will, like small children, stretch your hands outward and gradually lift yourselves upward into the lasting realms of Truth.

"Have faith in your God and work in such a way that this faith becomes alive, and the confines of ignorance which have, in the past, bound you to Terra, will be broken down and you will be able to crawl your way through the Universe.

"Thank you for your kind attention.

"Good afternoon to you all."

Transmission delivered by The Master Aetherius on December 28th, 1969 (Earthyear 6.174), through Doctor Shri Yogiriji George King.

The action reported by the Cosmic Master Aetherius must have been a bright glory to behold!

Here was the Hand of the veritable Creator Itself working towards the advancement of Its own more menial expressions; and minds and bodies alike, as parts of Its expression, were moved upwards along the long Karmic road of experience which eventually must end in God-like perfection.

As far as the long-suffering Logos of the Planet Earth was concerned, She, in order to protect the unevolved life forms upon Her glorious surface, had to withhold the energies given during Her Initiation and was therefore not able to fully express Herself as She should have been. The report of Her Initiation, while being so Holy and glorious as to be beyond our description, was, at the same time, **surely one of the saddest stories in the history of the Planet Earth!**

However, minute by minute, the pressures exerted by the Divine Law of Karma must keep all living entities, within its framework, in perpetual motion. From choice, life forms either involve or evolve — but cannot remain static. Eventually, pressures exerted by this all-pervasive Law of God must force even a Logos to take Her rightful position in the Heavens. The Logos Of Earth can either do this quickly or proceed more slowly, which is obviously the way that She, for the time being, intends to cooperate with these Karmic pressures. But one thing above everything else is an absolute certainty, and that is, in one way or another, She will have to cooperate with the all-pervasive, ever-evolving direction determined by the Karmic Law. All men should become aware of this for it constitutes the most important single problem facing all life streams upon the Planet Earth today!

If you are not advanced enough to do anything about a world-wide problem such as this it will not mean much to you, but if you are enlightened enough to at least try to help to solve it, you would not sleep too easily at night until you had formulated some type of a workable plan. If, as well as this, you had been instructed, as The Aetherius Society was ordered, to start an Operation which, although only in a small degree, would nevertheless assist The Logos Of Terra in the gradual release of this massive energy reserve, then you would know that you had to do something constructive about it.

On March 15th, 1965 (Earthyear 1.251), The Master Aetherius gave a Transmission, through myself, stating that The Aetherius Society had to build a Shape Power Temple which must include a mechanism capable, among other things, of acting as a "Power Stabilization Station." Full particulars and explanation of this important Transmission were published in The Aetherius Society Newsletters. (Note 11.)

The Aetherius Society is not a large, rich organization. Because our teachings are as advanced as they are, we are relatively small. Because of our size and the fact that we spend most of our finances on public service Missions for the benefit of mankind, unlike many organizations which spend most of their funds on profit-returnable items in one way or another, which we do not do; therefore to wait until we were in a financial position which allowed us to build the first Temple would, in my estimation, greatly hold up the next important step which we were committed to take.

On August 26th, 1967 (Earthyear 4.50), we were again reminded of these commitments by the Cosmic Master Aetherius, Who gave a vitally important Transmission called, "The Five Temples Of God." In this Transmission, the Cosmic Master suggested that we did not have to wait until the Shape Power Temple was built in order to start this "Power Stabilization Station." This vitally important Transmission, concerning directives given to The Aetherius Society for the next 1,000 years, together with a paragraph-by-paragraph explanation of this vitally important Cosmic Message, appears in a book, *The Five Temples Of God*, published by The Aetherius Society. (Note 12.) Although we had already worked this out, the confirmation came as a great relief to all of us who were wise enough to be led by greater Beings than ourselves.

Once again I approached, through concentration, contemplation and meditation, that all-knowledge Space of Divinity within and was able to design an apparatus capable of the functions which were previously dictated. After this I applied for an audience with, and had the great honour of being granted this audience, The Holy Lords Of The Ineffable Flame Of The Logos Of Earth. (Note 13.)

Part of the downfall of man has been brought about because he did not make the correct petitions to Higher Authority before he made his murderous atom bombs and tested them; before he dammed up rivers for his own use; before he cut tunnels through mountains to enable him to travel more quickly from place to place; and many other alterations to the Earth's surface. All this without gaining permission from The Great Lords. If you need proof of compassion shown by a Mighty Logos, then surely this is the most solid and logical proof which could ever be offered to any of you. Bear in mind, the great Cosmic Master Who lived on Earth in a terrestrial body Whom you called Jesus, stated, in reference to The Goddess Terra, these significant words:

"She has not as yet demanded that you change or leave."

The full text of the Twelve Transmissions given by The Master Jesus is printed verbatim in a book called, *The Twelve Blessings*, and published by The Aetherius Society. (Note 14.)

Not wishing to contravene the Divine Law, I approached The Protectors Of The Ineffable Flame Of The Logos Of Earth seeking permission to go ahead with the building of this apparatus in exactly the same way as I approached the same Lords before I started "Operation Sunbeam." I was told that the plans were acceptable, but not to incorporate any circuit in the apparatus which was designed to collect energies from the Earth until field research had been accomplished. (Note 15.)

A year and a half later, on July 28th, 1973 (Earthyear 10.21), a strange event took place which, although I did not realize it at the time, was due to provide a large piece added to the jigsaw puzzle of scientific discovery. Just previous to this, I had been engaged in a research project directly connected with the extension of ''Operation Sunbeam'' to the British Isles. Whilst in the Highlands of Scotland I had suffered a fall and sprained my ankle in a severe manner. I returned to the European Headquarters of The Aetherius Society in London and much to my frustration, had to remain in the Headquarters while the rest of the Staff and Members were enjoying a pilgrimage to a Holy Mountain called ''Holdstone Down'' in the north of Devonshire, some 250 miles away from London. During the evening of July 28th, equipment would be set up on ''Holdstone Down'' so that The Cosmic Masters could, from that place, invoke Spiritual Energies which, in turn, could be transmitted from ''Holdstone Down'' to the American Headquarters of The Aetherius Society in Los Angeles, 6,000 miles away. Specially trained operators in the Headquarters in America would then activate our sensitive astro-metaphysical receiver which was capable of unerringly picking up this stream of Spiritual Energy and putting it into one of our ''Operation Sunbeam'' batteries for later discharge into a Psychic Centre. Naturally, to miss an event like this, because of a previous accident, was, to say the least, most frustrating. However, now I can see that the giant, all-pervasive hand of Karma was at work.

Later this day, I received a desperate phone call from the ''Operation Sunbeam'' team in Devonshire. For the first time in all the years that ''Operation Sunbeam'' had been running, the team had forgotten an essential piece of equipment. They had dispatched a Staff Member, who was the owner of a fast motorcar and an excellent driver, back to the European Headquarters in order to collect this piece of equipment which was necessary for the correct alignment of apparatus capable of the transmission of Spiritual Energies to Los Angeles. In the meantime, because this Staff Member was in Devonshire and had a total journey of 500 miles to make, I dispatched another man from the European Headquarters with this equipment to expedite the delivery.

When you set a time to start an Operation of this nature, which involves Cosmic Masters, then you had better have your timing absolutely correct, there being no margin for error. The Staff Member arrived at the Headquarters — after what must have been a hectic drive — at approximately 1:00 p.m.

On the face of it, altogether a frustrating time.

An event which I dearly longed to take charge of had been denied my attendance because of a previous accident. Not only that, but again, to repeat for emphasis, for the first time, an essential piece of equipment had been left behind by the "Operation Sunbeam" team which, in the past, had never been guilty of such an omission.

Now, in order for the reader to fully understand the progress of this narrative, I must point out that the Staff Member in question was, by profession, an excellent draughtsman.

Even though I had been previously instructed by The Lords Of The Flame not to incorporate any circuit into the new Spiritual Energy Radiator capable of collecting energies previously given to The Logos Of Earth, later on this day I received a brilliant flash of illumination and was able to make a rough drawing of what I thought was an antenna system which I knew, at the time, had a wave form incorporated into it which was capable of the reception of Spiritual Energies which would be released by The Logos Of Terra at a later date. From my rough drawing and my answers to his repeated questions, my assistant, being a professional draughtsman, was able to make a good plan of, what was thought then to be, an antenna system.

In November 1979 (Earthyear 16), six years later, studying the plan in the light of deeper knowledge gained by the research programme into the improvement of "Operation Sunbeam," I was able to recognize this device which, if incorporated with a receiver coil which we had used with success in the old method of "Operation Sunbeam" throughout the years, was capable of the reception and controlled direction of energies released by The Logos Of Earth.

This was not only an antenna — but almost a complete collection and radiation device!

Now I can see very plainly why I was inspired to make the change in "Operation Sunbeam," because it was during the research, prior to this improvement of what was already in the eyes of Cosmic Beings, the most important Spiritual Mission on Earth today, that I discovered a potent way which could also be used later in our "Power Stabilization Station" — a much more definite procedure, by the way, than that originally designed for the apparatus for the future Shape Power Temple.

This discovery enabled us to perform one major function of the much larger apparatus, which still had to be built for the future Shape Power Temple. We were able to advance the whole project about six years as it was no longer necessary to wait until the large apparatus was built before initiating the "Power Stabilization Station."

I need no further proof above that which has happened repeatedly to me, to know that God does exist!

With this inner unshakeable knowledge, the realizer must then take the next step: *an unconditional surrender to God,* without thought of selfish likes or dislikes, without thought even of their own welfare. This *unconditional surrender* must be made, for only when it has been made is that person then capable of what must be called "modern miracles." During "Operation Sunbeam," because of this *unconditional surrender* made years before, I was able to learn some of the deeper secrets of the Planet. In the improvement of "Operation Sunbeam" I was able, not only to prove beyond any reasonable doubt what I already knew, but also to learn other deep secrets.

Dear readers, I call this — *"God's Magic in action!"*

There, virtually staring me in the face, was the answer to a problem which I had worked on many times during the past years and what is more, I had already begun to use the same procedure in the improved modus operandi of "Operation Sunbeam" which could now be used in a very effective, absolutely accurate way in the "Power Stabilization Station."

Indeed does God work in mysterious ways His Wonders to perform!

And thus the new Mission, "Operation Earth Light," built out of the tenuous matter of a heartfelt yearning, was given substance by meditative thought. "Operation Earth Light" suddenly became a living possibility, no, more than that — a living reality!

I must admit that there is more to this story on the history of the birth of "Operation Earth Light" than has been dealt with in this Chapter. As a matter of fact, the full story would fill a large tome. However, I feel it is sufficient, at this stage, to give to the reader these brief but important outlines leading up to the birth of this vitally important undertaking, "Operation Earth Light."

If you study the carefully chosen reference material recommended at the end of this Chapter you will discover that a most amazing story will unfold before you — one which will bring a deeper state of enlightenment to you all, and make you even more appreciative of the Holy Truths of life.

When an ignorant, uncouth mob, clay in the hands of an evil magician and manipulator, crucified one of the greatest Beings ever to set foot on this Planet — Jesus of Nazareth — the Being was allowed, by Karmic Law, to suffer His torment for a limited time only. Then, when apparently dead, He was taken from the cross of crucifixion. He rose again in an Ascended Body to prove there is no death — but only change.

I know from my researches and from information given to me by Elevated Beings, that The Logos of this Earth will only be allowed for a limited time — dictated by the Divine Law of Karma — to continue to hold Her Light under the crusty mantle of Her outside body. During this limited time She must, by the same Divine Law of Karma, make a gradual release of the Spiritual Energy given during Her Initiation. As the years go on, this release of energy, coming naturally through most of the 49 Psychic Centres within Her huge body, will increase.

It is not the purpose of my Mission, "Operation Earth Light," to interfere, in any way, with the natural release of energy from The Logos, for whatever I or you do — this will come, either with our help — or despite our lack of interest. However, being conversant with the deep occult factors concerning this, I feel that it is imperative to assist, even in a small way, this release of Spiritual Energy. This decision has been confirmed since, not only by the Elevated Being I regard as my own Master, but by The Protectors Of The Ineffable Flame Of The Goddess Herself. Apart from The Logos Herself, no Higher Authority lives on Earth today.

It must be pointed out to the reader that the Spiritual Energies given to The Logos Of Earth through the manipulations in "Operation Sunbeam" are in no way related to the massive Spiritual Energies which were given to The Logos by the Highest Powers in this Solar System during "The Initiation Of Earth." Although our

"Operation Sunbeam" is a very powerful Mission, the energy we are able to give back to The Logos is as a drop of water in an ocean when compared with the energy which The Logos has brought into physical manifestation on behalf of terrestrial man throughout the centuries. The fact that the Highest Powers gave permission for "Operation Sunbeam" and for the use of the improvement in our modus operandi, proves beyond any doubt, that in no way are we interfering with an energy balance. In fact, exactly the opposite. In our small way we are trying to preserve a Karmic balance through the manipulation of all-important Spiritual Energies. It is important for the reader to realize this fact.

If you visit a large supermarket to buy some food, you expect to pay for it, even though the shelves may be filled with foodstuffs. And yet, few people throughout the ages have made any real attempt to give even a small token repayment to The Logos Of Earth in return for Her continual manifestation in order to sustain mankind. As previously stated, "Operation Sunbeam" is a token repayment only on behalf of mankind and in no way affects or is related to the massive Spiritual Energy reserve now being held by The Logos, which was given during Her Primary Initiation on July 8th, 1964 (Earthyear 1.1).

AUTHOR'S RECOMMENDATIONS

NOTE 1. For more detailed information regarding the culture and philosophy of Beings Who reside on other Planets, read the book, *Life On The Planets*, published by The Aetherius Society. This popular publication is now in its fifth impression.

NOTE 2. For information regarding the advanced evolutionary status of the Cosmic Beings Who reside upon the Planet Saturn, the student is recommended to study Chapter 8 of the book, *The Nine Freedoms*, published by The Aetherius Society.

NOTE 3. For further details of "Operation Sunbeam," read *The Aetherius Society Newsletter*, Volume 5, Issues 10-12, May-June 1966; Issues 13-14, July 1966; Issues 15-17, August-September 1966; and Issues 18-20, September-October 1966.

Listen also to Metacassette® No. MC-2, *Operation Sunbeam Inspires The Galaxy*, for a detailed explanation by The Master Aetherius of the ramifications of "Operation Sunbeam." Also study Cassette No. C-54, *Operation Sunbeam*.

The history of this Mission has been recorded in *The Aetherius Society Newsletter* and Journal, *Cosmic Voice*. Details are obtainable from the publishers, The Aetherius Society.

NOTE 4. For information regarding the intervention in "Operation Sunbeam" by Masters from outside of this Solar System, listen to Metacassette® No. MC-19, *Gotha Speaks To Earth*. This is a unique Cosmic Transmission. Also read *The Aetherius Society Newsletter*, Volume 6, Issues 1-5, January-February 1967.

NOTE 5. For a vivid description of the elevated state, called in advanced occult circles, "Cosmic Consciousness," read Chapter 5 of the book, *The Nine Freedoms*, published by The Aetherius Society.

NOTE 6. For the details of the repercussions of "Operation Sunbeam" on the Planet Earth, read the amazing Revelations contained in the booklet, *Operation Sunbeam — God's Magic In Action*. This booklet also gives an account of the permission given by Doctor George King, the inventor of "Operation Sunbeam," to The Great White Brotherhood to perform "Operation Sunbeam."

Also read *The Aetherius Society Newsletter*, Volume 15, Issues 20-22, November 1976, for details of special Phases performed by The Great White Brotherhood and other Cosmic Forces.

NOTE 7. For full details of the first 21 Phases performed in the new aspect of "Operation Sunbeam," read *The Aetherius Society Newsletter*, Volume 18, Issues 29-32, November-December 1979.

For further information of the later 119 Phases of "Operation Sunbeam," read *The Aetherius Society Newsletter*, Volume 19, Issues 11-14, June-July, 1980; and *Cosmic Voice*, Volume 1, Issues 1-4, August-September 1980; Volume 2, Issues 7-8, May 1981; Volume 3, Issues 3-4, March, and Issues 8-10, September-October 1982; Volume 4, Issues 1-4, January-March, and Issues 9-12, July-September 1983; Volume 5, Issues 1-4, January-March 1984.

NOTE 8. For complete information on the stupendous event — The Primary Initiation Of Earth — read the book, *The Day The Gods Came*, which gives the Cosmic Transmission of this extraordinary metaphysical manipulation performed on July 8th, 1964. This book also contains a full explanation of this mighty Cosmic Event, with drawings to illustrate the procedure adopted by Highly Elevated Masters of Cosmic status. Close study of this great book is considered essential for all metaphysical students.

NOTE 9. For information and explanation of the different levels of existence around Earth, listen to Cassettes No. C-11, *Levels Of Consciousness — Part 1, The Spirit World;* No. C-12, *Levels Of Consciousness — Part 2, Realms Of The Masters;* and C-68, *Life After Death.*

Also read *The Three Saviours Are Here!* regarding life on the lower levels of existence, referred to as the "hells," published by The Aetherius Society. This information is unobtainable from any other source.

NOTE 10. The full account of the battle against alien forces on this Earth has not been published, but readers will receive some enlightening insight into the stupendous conflict engaged in by The Adepts for the protection of humanity through a study of *The Aetherius Society Newsletter*, Volume 4, Issue 16, August; Issues 20-24, October-December 1965.

Also read *The Three Saviours Are Here!* for information on "Operation Karmalight," another Mission of vital importance to the salvation of mankind.

NOTE 11. For details of the Cosmic Transmission entitled, "Let's Build That Temple," read *The Aetherius Society Newsletter*, Volume 4, Issues 8-9, April-May 1965.

NOTE 12. Read *The Five Temples Of God* — directives given to The Aetherius Society by The Master Aetherius for the coming 1,000 years — which gives details of the importance of the Shape Power Temples and their astro-metaphysical equipment.

NOTE 13. For further information regarding the meeting between Doctor George King and The Holy Lords Of The Ineffable Flame Of The Logos Of Earth, read *The Aetherius Society Newsletter*, Volume 11, Issue 1, January 1972; also Volume 11, Issues 9-10, July 1972, *A Visit To The Lords Of The Flame*.

NOTE 14. *The Twelve Blessings* is an extension of the Sermon on the Mount, which gives a Cosmic concept of life, as given by The Master Jesus. The book, *The Twelve Blessings*, not only contains some of the most profound Teachings ever given to Earth, but also forms a powerful metaphysical practice.

NOTE 15. Read *The Aetherius Society Newsletter*, Volume 11, Issue 1, January 1972, and Issues 9-10, July 1972, for information given to Doctor George King by The Lords Of The Ineffable Flame Of The Logos Of Earth, regarding further field research to be undertaken in connection with astro-metaphysical circuitry designed to pick up Spiritual Energies from The Logos Of Earth.

All the cassettes, books and Newsletters recommended above are currently available from the publishers, The Aetherius Society.

CHAPTER 2

THE LORDS
OF THE FLAME

To summarize the situation: we now had a workable plan which, when put into operation, would, I knew from previous research, enable the technical Staff of The Aetherius Society to build an apparatus, simple in design, which would answer the directive given in a Cosmic Transmission in 1970. But, so gigantic were the implications behind the process, that in order to ensure success, it was necessary for me now to gain permission before this plan could be implemented.

I left Los Angeles on November 14th, 1979 (Earthyear 16.130), and retired to my bungalow in Santa Barbara in order to prepare myself for the next essential step forward. Later that same day, I left my home in Santa Barbara at 1:28 p.m. and walked, alone, down Loyola Drive and down the steps onto the beach. It seems that I was fortunate in that the tide was out, for at full tide, this beach is covered.

This small span of beach, stretching approximately one mile to the point in Santa Barbara, is to me Holy, for occasionally in the past, have I walked along this narrow stretch, with the surf pounding in my ears on one side and the jagged, unpicturesque, fawn clay cliffs on the other side, but have been in a state of bliss for it is on this stretch of Holy beach where I have contacted my Master and felt His Love, compassion and understanding wrap me in the envelope of His Wisdom. The same experience was enjoyed this time.

As always, the approach to my request was gentle, yet firm. As always, His introduction was the same:

"I would attach myself to your consciousness, my son."

My spine grew cold as though it were frozen.

I staggered slightly in my walk.

Then, when my mind accepted the contact, I was in mental communication with a Being of great power, yet gentle compassion. I cannot do justice to the type of communication which passed mentally between us, save to say that in my blundering exuberance, I asked if He knew about "Operation Earth Light."

The answer was simple and to the point:

"Yes I do — continue."

I then put forward my ideas regarding the way that "Operation Earth Light" should be performed. I will not reveal exactly how this Mission will be performed at this stage, because such is the vastness of this Mission that I realize the scientific secrets appertaining to the modus operandi should be revealed only to a chosen few who have taken an oath of secrecy and allegiance to The Aetherius Society and to The Spiritual Hierarchy Of Earth for life — to keep the actual details of the modus operandi strictly secret.

I know this is right, despite what some of my readers may think.

One of the most health-giving properties of rock on the surface of Earth is natural radioactivity. This used wrongly, as it is by man, produces the killer atom bomb — and nuclear-tipped missiles. I have always said — although these statements have seldom been understood by the world — that the greatest good in the wrong hands can become the worst evil. Hence my care not to reveal the essence of the science behind the complete performance of "Operation Earth Light." Suffice it to say, a far greater Being than I, Whom I consider my Master to be, accepted the Mission with some enthusiasm.

He went on to tell me that the way I intended to perform "Operation Earth Light" was necessary at this stage, but I had to regard the Operation only as a pattern for others to follow; that our assistance in helping to release Spiritual Energies from The Logos would be a token only — but important because of its performance! He also revealed to me that the Spiritual Energies which passed through my apparatus, at certain given times during the year, would not affect mankind in a direct way but would be used by the Higher Devic Kingdom. (Note 1.)

As soon as this information was imparted I could see the perfection of a greater plan than that devised by myself — a plan so superb that it made me gasp in astonishment! Quickly my mind ran to our "Operation Sunbeam" in which energies from Holy places in the world, *originally meant for mankind*, were given in sacrificial action to The Logos; and our "Operation Prayer Power" in which energies invoked by Mantra and Prayer are sent to suffering people throughout the world. (Note 2.) And now, as if to dot the last "i" in perfect balance, here was a Mission which would help to convey Spiritual Energies to the Devas.

There is no more perfect balance that I can think of.

Spiritual Energies to The Logos as a Karmic manipulation.

Spiritual Energies to suffering mankind through "Operation Prayer Power" — which is a gigantic mass Healing tool.

And through "Operation Earth Light," Spiritual Energies sent to the Higher Devic Kingdom which, being close to nature in all Her multitudinous aspects, would give the Devas unconditioned power to use so that they could perform their functions as originally intended.

The balance was perfect.

But then — God, The Inspirer, is perfect.

During those few seconds or minutes of this realization — for I had no idea of time during this state — this concept came to me as a flash of dazzling illumination.

Unless you have been in this position not one of you can really appreciate how I felt. Not great, not powerful, as a king or an emperor; no, different — very different from that. I felt as though I had been used as a tool in the hands of greater Beings Who were working in a mysterious but definite way for the benefit of all men upon Earth.

Through "Operation Sunbeam" we manipulate the negative Karma of the world.

Through "Operation Prayer Power" we give mass Healing to suffering humanity.

Through "Operation Earth Light" we manipulate power to the Higher Devic Kingdom so that they can perform their functions without having to use the discoloured energies propelled towards them by the wrong thought impulses from the mass of humanity.

I surrender this to you all, in humility, as the most perfect plan of Service to others!

My Master then reminded me, as I knew He would, that before any start was made to tune in, by scientific means, to the Psychic Centre which, by the way, I had chosen and He agreed upon, I would have to approach The Master Babaji, Who is now the Spiritual Head of The Spiritual Hierarchy of this Earth. The Master Babaji would in turn seek from The Lords Of The Flame an interview on my behalf so that the final permission for the Mission could either be granted or refused by The Lords as They deemed fit.

After imparting this truly uplifting information to me, my Master gave me His Blessings and then, in a gentle but definite manner, detached His mental thoughts from my consciousness.

Another definite step towards making "Operation Earth Light" a living reality had been taken! A step which was not only successful but had taught me many things about the future of this important project.

I returned to my home at approximately 2:30 p.m. on November 14th, 1979 (Earthyear 16.130), having, in that hour, lived through an uplifting experience which I find very difficult to describe in such a way as to do justice to it.

My next move was to approach The Master Babaji Himself. Although He was a Being of prominent station, this was one of the easiest parts of the whole process. Before now, on more than one project, I have worked hand-in-hand with this Master and He probably knows me better than I know myself.

On the verge of something great — beware!

The days which followed were days of utter frustration for me.

Among other things I broke a tooth, exposing the nerve and could not eat solid food for five days. Bear in mind, I was not going out to an ordinary job in an ordinary office; my strength was needed more than ever before — and I knew it! I realized that it was my responsibility, if an audience was granted with The Lords Of The Flame, to make the dangerous journey to the centre of the Earth and back safely, for They are lodged deep in the core of this Planet. If I was incapable of this task then surely I did not deserve an audience with these great Beings. Some of you may not agree with my logical approach but nevertheless, it is the correct one.

After sitting for too many horrific hours in a dentist's chair, the injections which the dentist was forced to use completely upsetting the delicate balance of my constitution, and after having my wife suddenly taken ill with bronchitis and being afflicted myself with "stomach flu," I was still determined to go through with it.

Despite my pain and suffering, I approached The Master Babaji Who made the initial approach on my behalf.

The Lords Of The Ineffable Flame agreed to meet me.

So, on November 28th, 1979 (Earthyear 16.144), we left Los Angeles — myself, my wife and a male Staff Member — and proceeded to Santa Barbara in preparation for my astral projection and appearance before The Mighty Lords.

On the morning of November 29th the weather in Santa Barbara was beautiful; the temperature was a little high for the time of the year, but the air was so clear that one could easily see the islands 20 miles away. I walked around the small grounds of my little house and was delighted to see how green everything looked for November. Then I went back into the house again, into a room regarded as my study, and opened the chrome clasps on a dark green oblong box, threw the lid open and carefully turned on the main valve of the oxygen tank which was housed therein. I took out the black breathing mask, slipped the elastic around the back of my head, turned the main tap on and made a test. After making the test successfully and finding that, above the recommended dose of seven litres, I could breathe the oxygen quite freely without strain, I shut off the green tap on the top of the oxygen tank and left the lid open. I then informed my wife and my assistant that the oxygen apparatus had been tested and was ready. I hoped sincerely that this would not be needed — but remember, I intended to make a division between the physical counterpart of myself and the auric counterpart, the latter being the body in which I would travel deep down into the very core of Earth to meet Three Majestic Beings Who were vastly my superiors.

The time was 11:30 a.m. Pacific Standard Time. Despite the fact that my wife was ill and at that time I was suffering with a

condition which can be termed as ''stomach flu,'' I was still determined to go ahead with the meeting as it had been prearranged for
12:00 noon Pacific Standard Time, on this day, November 29th,
1979 (Earthyear 16.145).

Already my assistant had set up a tiny transmitter which
needed only a slight pressure from my finger to convey a warning
to him and my wife, both of whom were sitting quietly in the main
drawing room. I walked into my bedroom, tested the buzzer and
received confirmation from the others that this was working.

All projection from the human body is dangerous.

A projection of this kind was even more dangerous than that
undertaken by most Yogis and I knew it only too well!

Hence the buzzer system so that, immediately upon my return,
the others could be alerted to come to my assistance with oxygen
and Spiritual Healing if necessary.

After all, the whole idea behind the projection was that it should
be successful and not that I should become a cripple for life, for
this would have defeated its own purpose.

I had to gain permission for the commencement of ''Operation
Earth Light'' and had to be in an Earth physical body afterwards
to make sure that the Operation was performed according to my
original design. It is easy to die — often more difficult to live.
Those of you who have not been in such a position will not understand this statement but believe me, it is a statement of Truth.

I was very conscious of the fact that upon my shoulders lay the
acceptance and therefore the commencement of ''Operation Earth
Light'' — or its rejection. I did suffer from what may be commonly termed as ''stage fright.'' It is said, in acting circles, that
the best actors always have ''stage fright'' before their first
appearance. This was not the first time I had contacted The
Mighty Lords Of The Flame but probably because of my undermined health condition and maybe even age — I have to be honest
and admit it — it seemed that I suffered worse ''stage fright'' this
time than before. Or maybe it was because, from experience,
I now realized the greatness of these Beings far more than ever
before. Whatever it was, my stomach tightened up into knots to
such an extent that before lying down I had to relieve the muscu-
lar spasms in the solar plexus region by vigorous massage. There

was something due to happen of a more advanced nature this time than before because I had been informed by The Master Babaji, after He had gained permission for this audience on my behalf, that I had to wear special protective clothing and arrangements had been made so that I could be so attired.

The time was now 11:40 a.m. Pacific Standard Time.

A little room on the mesa in Santa Barbara. Two walls covered with bright-flowered patterns of pink and green and red and cream. Two other walls covered with pink stripes finding their unwavering way across a cream background. This striped pattern was broken by four doors leading to cupboards behind, papered bright green. Blue carpet. Sunlight outside. Warmth — gentle, creeping, lulling me into a state of false security.

When I drew the red curtains across the windows, in order to cut out most of the light, the runners on the curtain tracks seemed to make far more noise than ever before.

I had already changed into comfortable garments and was ready to lie on my bed so that the posture would be straight and comfortable and therefore devoid of unnatural strain. I lay on the bed, half rolled over, touched the buzzer button and heard my loyal companions answer immediately from a room farther down the hallway.

Now it is all up to me.

I started my deep breathing and Mantra practices in order to control my thoughts. At first this was not easy, for the first thing that became evident was my physical discomfort. It is strange, but at that time I thought about another Operation, performed many years ago, called "Operation Starlight." In this Mission I climbed 18 mountains throughout the world in order to act as a channel so that these mountains could receive an initial Charge of Spiritual Energy given by Cosmic Intelligences, thereby making them Holy for all time. (Note 3.) I was lecturing on "Operation Starlight" and after the lecture, a well-meaning but ill-informed lady came to me and said:

"Well, Doctor King, it must have been a lot easier for you on those mountains than your comrades because you obviously did not feel the blizzard that you described."

I remember looking at this innocent, but I am sorry to have to say it, ignorant face, and shaking my head and saying:

"Madam, if I had not felt that blizzard far more acutely than my comrades, then they would have been chosen as the channels through whom the Charge was made, and not me!"

I will never forget the look of pain which came over that lady's face when she suddenly realized the Truth. When one is sensitive, one is more aware of what is happening around them than an insensitive person. A slight movement to a sensitive person means far more than the same movement would to the insensitive person. Straightforward logic but little understood or appreciated.

When I lay down, perfectly still, I became far more acutely aware of my pains than had been apparent during my more basic preparations for the task ahead.

The secret is to divorce oneself completely from one's surroundings.

Somewhere a dog was barking. It seemed a long way away — but not far enough.

Despite the fact I was reciting my Mantra in silent earnestness I could not help thinking about — at first mundane things — and then later about the greater, more important happenings. I have always believed that under certain conditions you can live a quarter of a lifetime in a few minutes. I now know this to be true beyond any doubt. If one is perfectly honest with oneself, and you must be, your mind will dwell upon your weaknesses and then if you force it to, the better parts of your character which, again, can and do, under certain conditions, appear to be in themselves a weakness in one way or another. I knew this, having projected from the physical structure many times in the past — and purposely threw my thoughts outward to dwell upon the Earth Itself. The velocity of thought inside the human frame is about 650 miles per hour. The velocity of thought outside of the human body, when directed in the correct manner through deep concentration and predetermination, is many times the speed of light.

My thoughts sped like mental hounds released upon the hunt, across the beautiful surface of this truly gorgeous Planet. Seas — blue, deep, moving, iridescent. Ice — cold, jagged, glistening brightly in the sunshine. Mountains — dark brown, precipitous, decorated by white tips. Deserts — like dry biscuits, under the sweltering sunlight. Green valleys — procreating from themselves as trees reached upward as though like green, living flames reaching for their God. Cities — murky beneath shrouds of blue-green gas created by themselves. Lakes — placid, blue, dancing in the sunlight or tossing their white heads in answer to ever-blowing winds. Flat plains — covered by ragged stubble — the remains of golden crops. There was the vastness of seas, the loneliness of cragged mountains, the intimacy of green forests, the usefulness of crops, the aridness of deserts — and people, people everywhere — with hopes, likes, dislikes, despair, sadness and joy — everywhere this mass of humans was moving across the surface of this great Planet; improving, destroying, hopeful and hopeless alike, they moved, a great mass, a multitude of people. People, for the most part, whose very essence, whose very God-like Divinity, was hidden deep within recesses forged by their everyday existence. People who brought gladness to me, who brought sadness to me, who brought no hope to me as I shared, for one fleeting moment, their utter despair, for these had not developed the inner realization of the glory of the God in Which they dwelt.

Despite my control — tears welled up in my eyes for them.

I would like to have stopped that meditation and been given the powers to speak to every man, woman and child, afflicted with despair upon the surface of this Planet, and tell them how wrong they were, that they were Sparks of the Divine, here to learn their lessons in a truly glorious classroom. Although this had been said throughout the centuries by many before, most of the seeds of Wisdom which such philosophy planted have fallen on arid ground.

I will tell you, the road to enlightened success must pass through the dark valleys of sadness before the mountains of accomplishment can be climbed!

Such pity and compassion for mankind did I have at that time, had this meditation not been the prelude to a more elevated state which was designed to help man, I would have aborted it . . . !

But I had to continue — I had to.

Some ancient prompting, greater than even my sublime thoughts, seemed to be directing me unerringly towards a predetermined destination, as though some all-knowing mental hand was beckoning me onwards — onwards and outwards — outwards — outwards...!

When this full realization came it was followed by a glorious freedom.

No longer did I feel the pains and limitations of that poor aging body lying in the back room of a bungalow in California but, as though the world — no, not only the world — but Space stretched before me.

Immediately I found myself in a familiar type of saucer-shaped craft and was happy to be there.

I could see the gold-white-black-magenta-green panels in the rounded walls of the craft and seemed to be able to take in these sights in a fleeting second, which I should have been able to do because of — familiarity. Although I was in an auric body those Five Beings in this Spacecraft seemed as real to me as I was to Them. Two of Them came forward with a specialized type of a suit which I was informed mentally, was the protective garment which had to be worn by direction of The Lords Themselves. I recognized these Two Beings as Two of The Adepts to Whom mankind owes so very much for the direct help which They have rendered to suffering humanity in the past. (Note 4.)

A quick glance and recognition of the other Three registered in the same way. One of the Two Who approached me in humanoid form, was gigantic, standing almost seven feet in height, with massive broad shoulders and a chest which would put a weightlifter's to shame, and was easily recognizable as the Adept Who goes under the simple pseudonym of "Nixies Zero Zero Three." The Other, much smaller, wearing an oriental countenance, was also well known to me by the simple name of "Nixies Zero Zero Two."

I was dressed, with Their help, in a garment which appeared to be made of a type of plastic, extremely flexible, very comfortable to get into and covered me from a little below the ankles, and the uniform was finished with a tight collar around the neck made of the same silvery-coloured material. After this, certain instruments were clipped onto holders on the outside of the protective suit and it was explained very briefly — with a slight smile

TYPICAL SPACECRAFT AS USED BY THE ADEPTS

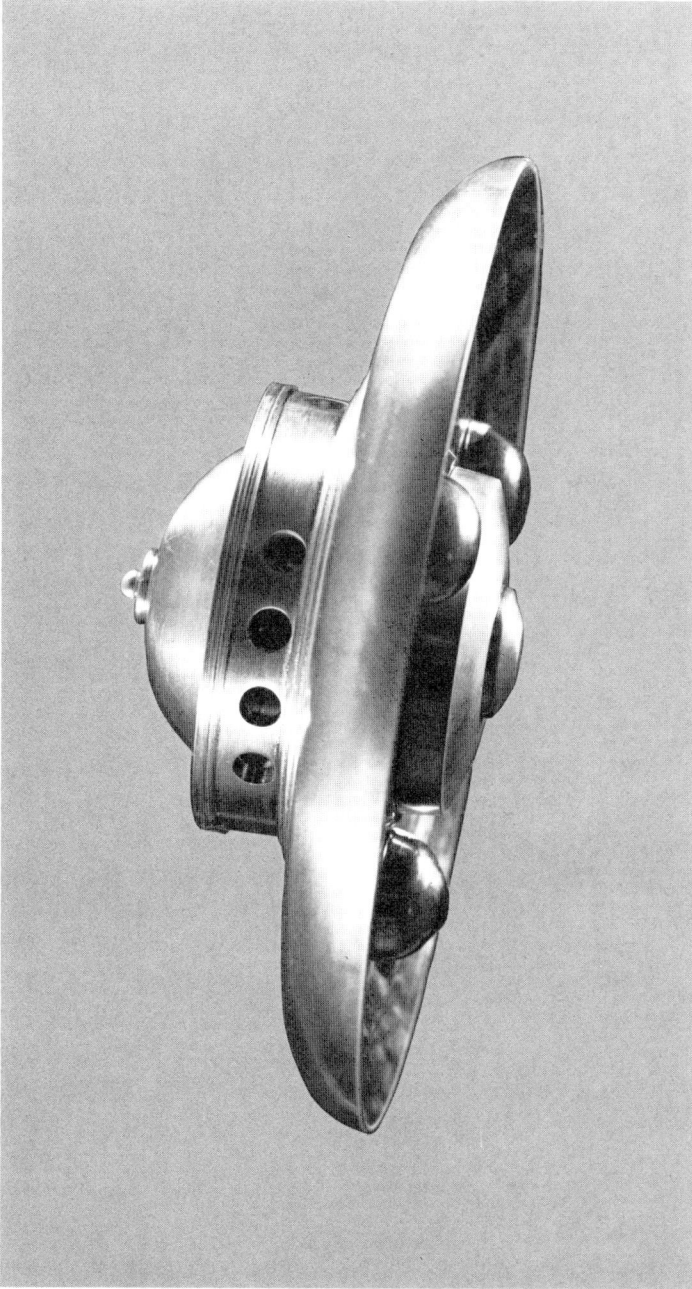

An illustration of a model of a Spacecraft made from information obtained from several reliable sources by the author. Although not an exact replica of the Spacecraft used by The Adepts to convey the author to his destination, it does give a good idea of the basic external characteristics of the aeroform.

on the faces of the Two Adepts — how these worked. As for the
boots, I told Them that I was capable of putting these on myself,
or I had better abort the Mission. Although Interplanetary in
origin, Three of those Adepts, having lived on the Planet Earth
for some time, were familiar with what we might term a terrestrial
sense of humour. I think we all laughed at this comment, especially since the Others put a different meaning on it than most
readers will.

Meanwhile, the craft had gathered momentum, although I did
not feel any G-force whatsoever, and we were heading for a
mysterious island called — Britain. When we arrived in the south
of England it was dark and the landing was made without any
show of lights so as not to arouse too much public concern about
what could be commonly termed as a "Flying Saucer landing,"
on the well-known Salisbury Plain, a few miles from the world-
famous Stonehenge and not far from the site of a massive Temple
which, now ancient and in ruins, was built near Avebury.

Of the four entrances to the core of Earth, this was by far the
easiest to traverse once one had made the transition into the subtle
tube-like entrance itself and this entrance was less dangerous
than taking any of the other three entrances. The moorland surrounding that entrance, which led deep down where The Lords
dwell, is probably the most valuable real estate in the world today,
if Britain did but know it.

The Spacecraft and The Adepts were in the same subtle frequency range which I was in and therefore everything seemed to
me just as physical as would people in a supermarket. Because
of the frequency framework it was necessary for Them to open
a sliding panel in the side of the Spacecraft and drop the outside
force screens before I could disembark. Just before I left the
Spacecraft, One of the Beings Whom I recognized as the Spiritual
Head of The Spiritual Hierarchy Of Earth, The Lord Babaji Himself, came to me and whispered some words of advice for which
I was later very thankful. Then, in terrestrial language, They all
mentally wished me good fortune and I disembarked onto the wet,
soggy moorland of this hillock.

According to my chronometer the time was 19:55 hours Green-
wich Mean Time. I did not hear the panel in the side of the Space-

craft close behind me — but rather felt it.

I was suddenly alone — very much alone.

The plans which I had to offer to The Lords were lodged in my memory because I knew Them to be well versed in the science of mental telepathy and felt that I should be well prepared. I also felt something else — and felt it very deeply. In my meditations, just a short time before in another part of the world, I had taken a view of the mightiness of this Planet. Now I was going to see Three Beings Who, while not a part of The Logos, or Life Form, of this Planet, nevertheless did act in the most trusted position on the Planet, that of protecting the Ineffable Flame which was the Life Force of the mighty Goddess Terra — on which I stood.

Suddenly my plans appeared to be very small and very, very insignificant.

The more practical, basic side of myself told me to turn around and go back.

Here I was coming with a good idea, but what an insignificant way of crystallizing that idea into definite action. Admittedly, I had many accomplishments in my corner, so to speak: that of the improvement of "Operation Sunbeam," allowing the Masters to put more Spiritual Energy into The Logos than before; that of "Operation Starlight"; that of "Operation Bluewater" — to mention just a few. (Note 5.) But now to ask for a special audience with The Mighty Ones Themselves and to be able to offer Them such trivial nonsense as the plans for the apparatus to start the "Power Stabilization Station" which were now lodged in my mind, was an action which tested my confidence to the very limit — I can tell you. It seems that the more you do, the more you become aware of what you can do and this sapped every ounce of confidence from me at that time. All right, no one else on Earth had thought about it, but how did I intend to do it? Was it in the best way possible to me or was I taking a short cut which could not be permitted?

And then the gentle beckoning "voice" cut through my undermined consciousness. I could do naught else but follow that "voice." It did not come from inside of myself but from outside — in a gentle, delicately inviting manner. As though I were a desert plant being nourished by the waters from the skies above.

A great strength flowed into me and gave an added determination which surprised me at the time. I reached up and pressed firmly on a small button in a belt around my waist — and the ground disappeared from view. I had altered my vibratory rate, with the help of the special equipment in the garment, so was able to enter the subtle entrance tube which led to my destination.

At first, the darkness of the night outside changed to even blacker darkness within this entrance. All I could see was the slight flickering blue-white radiance which I knew to be a magnetic emanation from the protective garment I wore. I seemed to be swallowed up by the very Earth — which, of course, was true.

Down, down I travelled.

I do not know how long it took precisely; I do not know what speed was reached or what depth was penetrated before I saw the light. Deep red, ruddy light seemed to shine out of the pitch stygian blackness which, at first, penetrated even the garment, until I had sense enough to activate a control on the neckband of the helmet which I had been warned to do by The Master Babaji Himself. Looking to one side at a gauge in the protective clothing, I could see that the temperature outside of my private little world had risen to 2,019° centigrade. Whereas my body, completely covered by this garment — a magnificent engineering feat in its own right — was kept at a temperature which was bearable to me. Keep in mind, I was in an auric body and not a physical one. The temperature inside the suit would have been very uncomfortable for a physical structure because the skin, by now, would have blistered, exposing the near-to-the-surface blood vessels. But the aura, being in some ways denser, and yet at the same time, more tenuous, is capable of standing outside pressures which would crush a physical structure and the same laws apply to outside temperatures, either high or low. Nevertheless, I was very thankful to be clothed by Beings Who realized the difficulty of this journey. I was travelling through a subtle energy tube which passed straight through the mysterious magma level of this Planet. The ruddy glow subsided and a soft, cold, silver fluorescence appeared outside of the tube down which I passed.

In the greatest good there is also the worst danger.

I knew that I was now passing through the very arteries of this

Planet in which She stores vast Spiritual and magnetic energies to dispense these through Her complex nervous system from the surface to the very core itself. This is the most valuable element on Earth, bar none. If one tries to penetrate this fluidic layer of, shall we call it, ''element X'' at the wrong time, one's auric structure will be torn apart by vast energies which pass, in concentrated pulses, through this life blood, from near the surface of the Planet right down to Her very Heart. As blood is to a human, so ''element X'' is to The Logos Of The Planet Earth. By far the most powerful element on Earth in its natural fluidic state, it has been sought many times by people not advanced enough to be able to control it and they have died as a result. In one part of the world some years ago, scientists were seeking this element in a deep cave, and not only did they meet an untimely end, but the reaction caused by their interference resulted in an earthquake in that area which killed thousands of people!

This element has tides, like a sea, which are excited at certain times of the year and during these periods of excitation, the flow is greatly speeded up by the energy release from the element itself. If this element was isolated and controlled, then it would cure disease in human bodies on Earth. By the same token, in its natural, moving state, like radioactivity, it will kill, but in a more devastating way. As any metaphysician, worthy of the title knows, radioactivity operates on seven levels of existence, the same as light, and in a concentrated form, can affect the seven bodies of man. This element is similar, only in a concentrated form, the effects will be even more pronounced. (Note 6.)

As I stated earlier, if I were not capable of making the journey through the Earth to The Lords, then I did not deserve Their attention.

But the tube, formed by some powerful magnetic construction of which I am ignorant, and the garment I was wearing, protected me adequately from any detrimental effects this powerfully pulsing element may have had upon my auric structure.

Then the change from complete blackness, through molten magma, through the bright silvery opalescence of ''element X,'' suddenly stopped and I found myself in a vast room.

I instantly became aware of a figure standing before me,

dressed in a dark robe with a hood which obscured his face completely. He was about my size and looked quite humanoid in every way, save for the rather weird characteristic of this hood obscuring his face completely. He beckoned to me.

I followed.

With a quick glance around I could see that the room was very high, if room it was, and way up near the ceiling there were some glowing spheres of silvery light which did not light the whole room as would electric lights on Earth, but gave one the strange ability to see just as easily as one would if walking through a brilliantly illuminated terrestrial office, but without being conscious of the light itself. It was as though these moving spheres had the ability to enhance one's eyesight — probably by subtle manipulation on the brain centres — to such an extent that one could see like a cat in the darkness — and yet not even that.

As soon as I began to follow, in terrestrial fashion, behind my guide, whose face I still had not seen, I felt a pronounced lightness of the body and discovered that I was no longer touching the floor but rather whisked just over the surface of the ground in a levitated state. But the levitation had not been brought on by myself but came from outside of myself, as though some guiding hand were moving me in a determined, swift manner towards an objective. As we started to move in this fashion, the illuminating spheres came further down from the very high ceiling above and followed us. It was very unearthly to say the least, even though I was nearer to the greatest aspect of Earth than most men have ever been.

I do not exactly know what distance was covered in this strange, almost weird flight, following the dark clad figure in front with a cluster of small, shining silvery fluorescent spheres behind, but the journey abruptly ended and, at the same time, I felt myself gently settle down onto my feet.

Suddenly Three Figures appeared in front of me.

I did not see Them enter — They just appeared...!

These were The Protectors Of The Ineffable Flame Of The Logos Of The Planet Earth!

I had known, from previous experience, that these Three Mighty Beings were either Interplanetary or Intergalactic in origin; that They were providing an essential Service to Earth and mankind which crawled its way through habitation upon the surface. Nevertheless, probably for my sake, They appeared in what seemed to be similar bodies to an earthman — in shape, that is — but there the similarity ended. At a mental request from One of Them, I slipped my right hand underneath an almost concealed lever on the side of my neckband, pulled and turned it slightly and without any more effort, the helmet came loose and I took it from my head. In a projected state one can live for certain lengths of time without breathing gas through one's nostrils or mouth, providing one can absorb similar life-giving energy through the psychic centres in one's body. However, if there is gas, such as an oxygen-nitrogen mixture present and that gas is impregnated with certain other energies, such as those found on the surface of Earth, it makes existence, even in an auric structure, a lot more straightforward. I was amazed by the fact that there was an atmosphere down here and an atmosphere which seemed to be charged with life-supporting energies more pronounced than the atmosphere at the seaside during a summer's morning on the surface!

The Three Beings in front of me had similar facial characteristics. Each of Them was dressed in a bright magenta-coloured robe. Oddly enough, I did not become immediately aware of this until I stared hard at Them. It seemed that the robe itself was capable of picking up characteristics from the Life Form it covered, for the harder I looked at this garment, the brighter it became. They wore no other adornments which I was aware of at that time. Each of Them seemed to be about seven feet tall, with long silver hair which fell down to Their shoulders. They were clean shaven. The eyes of all of Them seemed to be the same shape, very slightly slanted, not as much as an oriental on Earth, but nevertheless, the slant was there. Their eyes appeared to me, to be brown in colour. Immediately I thought of this, Their eyes changed colour to a bright blue for a second and then back to brown again. I had learned a lesson — not to make definite conclusions regarding these Beings, except one obvious one, that was the fact that They could undoubtedly form a body of any shape They wished, whenever They wished, depending on prevailing conditions, and, I felt strongly, a taste of compassion and good manners on Their part.

One of Them turned sideways, waved His hand and the large room — or was it a cave — sprang into brilliant light. So brilliant that even my psychic eyes were dazzled, for a moment, before they became adjusted to it. The light did not appear to come from any concentrated bright source but emanated from thousands of globes which floated overhead and had the same strange ability as the other spheres I had seen, namely, to afford illumination while the source, the globe itself, seemed to be fairly dim. To light a room of that apparent size, for I never saw its full size, in that way would have been impossible upon Earth. The lights were not hidden, but in full view and when one looked at them, they glowed, but not excessively brightly, and yet, their reaction was such as to brilliantly illuminate this vast enclosure.

I was in a projected state and could only remain in this state for a given time without physical and mental danger to my dense counterpart back on the surface. The Lords knew this because, without hesitation, I was requested to follow Them. The Three of Them turned and I followed towards what looked like another empty space in this room, for as yet, I had seen no furnishings whatsoever, or decoration for that matter.

As They walked, a table and four high-backed carved chairs suddenly appeared in front of the Three Beings.

As if to put me at ease, for I felt that They could have walked straight through the table and chairs — They did not do so but arranged Themselves on one side of this table, remained standing and mentally invited me to unfasten my garment and seat myself on the opposite side. I accepted the invitation. No sooner had I done so, than another hooded figure, whose face was covered like the first one, appeared. I said another one, because this one wore the same dark-coloured garment, except that, unlike the first one, he wore around his middle a bright yellow sash. He put, what looked at first like a writing pad, in front of One of The Lords Who passed His hand across it three times from left to right and then handed it to me. He actually pushed it across the table to me.

I took one glance at it and nearly fell from my chair...!

I gaped across at Him for a moment, eyes wide with astonishment, and received a compassionate, understanding, knowing smile in answer to my stumbling mental request. There, on this piece of what looked like crystalline sheet in front of me, was a drawing — an exact replica of the one drawn in 1973 in London — even the colours were the same, by the way — of the so-called antenna unit!

"Do not be alarmed," I heard in my mind; *"This design was prevalent in your thought pattern and simply translatable."*

In a matter of a few moments, this Being had read my thoughts so completely that He could reproduce them, with three small gestures of His hand, upon this crystalline slate. Although I have had the honour of meeting The Lords Of The Flame on previous occasions, this is the first time that this ability was demonstrated to me. In the past, the meetings have been brief, an exchange of mental picturizations and an affirmative answer. But this time, The Lords, probably out of compassion for my insistence, intended to go further.

"Move your hand and wipe it clean and then think about your procedure," came the mental order — delivered firmly but with a kind gentleness.

I did move my hand and was amazed to see that the crystal slate came clean after doing so. I then thought about the main aspect of the modus operandi for ''Operation Earth Light'' and the main reason for my audience with The Lords. When this had been done, again I was amazed that a full picturization, exactly as it had been thought, even to a large knot tied in a rope, by the way, appeared on the slate.

If you can swallow in an auric body, I did so — and hard.

I carefully turned the crystal slate around and moved it over to the Being sitting between the other Two. I think it was to put me at ease that the Three of Them looked at it. Now I come to recall afterwards, I do not think any of Them needed to have looked at what was drawn there by my mental impulses, although They did so and passed it back with a statement of permission:

"You may proceed with this plan. You are cognizant of

*the fact this 'Operation Earth Light' of yours, while having
Our full sanction, must be regarded as a pattern only for the
time being. Others will follow this pattern.*

*"We thank you for your thought, consideration and com-
passion for mankind by formulating this essential plan in
these troubled times.*

"Proceed with Our Blessings."

To say I was happy about this does not do justice to my feelings.

All right, in 1956 I had been to the moon and was able to tell scientists that when they landed men upon the moon they would discover an alien base there. (Note 7.) In 1979 the truth was revealed
that an alien base was discovered on the moon by several astro-
nauts during one of the Space probes made there. That is one
thing; it is another thing entirely to formulate a Mission as big as
"Operation Earth Light" and have permission to proceed from
such an Authority as Those Who had just granted it! It is one thing
to be able to talk about advanced concepts of mind 15 years ago,
and those concepts being gradually "discovered" by science today, which I have done; it is another thing to sit somewhere, deep
down in the bowels of a Planet, and have Beings of this calibre
give you the go-ahead on a plan which you had devised.

My reminiscences were broken when I was invited to, believe
it or not, ask some questions. I looked around the vast hall in
which we sat, devoid of any other furnishings save the chairs and
the table, and the ever-present spheres of light glowing high above
my head, and mentally asked where I was. The answer came back
immediately:

*"We are now 3,226¼ miles beneath a part of Scotland
you know well. In fact, straight above our heads is the mountain called 'Ben Hope'."* (Note 8.)

"So much for science's idea of a solid-core Earth," I managed
to reply.

"Orthodox science is as a child learning his alphabet,"
was the mental reply.

"And so is terrestrial metaphysical science," I repeated.

The Three agreed with me.

Then there was a silence for a short time while another helper appeared, attired in the same way, except this time, he had a white sash around the middle of his dark-coloured garments. He reached over and took the crystal slate from the table. If you had asked me if he grasped the slate, which was quite heavy, and picked it up as a humanoid would, I would have to say that I did not see him do this. It was as though, when his hands were near to the slate, the slate moved into his hands, rather than him picking it up. I must have expressed surprise at noticing this and brought out the next question, addressing the Three of Them:

"My Lords, how many helpers do You have?"

The answer should have surprised me but it did not.

"As many as We need. You see, there are only Three of Us down here."

There was a pause so that this information could sink in and allow me to understand the implications of the apparent contradiction.

"So these helpers are 'shades' manufactured by Two or probably Three of You. The coloured sashes, or absence of a sash, would denote Who has thought the 'shade' into being. Am I right?" I asked.

"That is correct," I was informed mentally.

"Where do You Lords come from?" I asked.

"All in good time," was the answer to that one.

"Now, as you are in a state which terrestrials refer to as projection, it is time, and you are governed by this, that you left. But before you do depart, I would like to give an affirmative answer to one question I know you will ask, either now or in the future."

It should be quite obvious to everyone what question I would have asked had I been bold enough to phrase it in thought, and that is: "Would it be possible for me to know more about The Logos?"

Believe it or not, The Lords anticipated such a brazen question from yours truly and agreed that, at some future date, this would be possible. Why? Who knows. Probably out of compassion on Their part, or probably because They felt that this knowledge should be imparted to many through one like myself. I feel it was a collection of both of these factors which brought this affirmative answer and with it, an invitation to return.

The Three of Them arose and, to my surprise, bowed very slightly to me and I returned the bow, almost hitting my head on the table top as I did so.

"Your exit will be swifter than your entrance. Do return carefully and soon," I was requested in a way that sounded more like a gentle order.

Now the four of us stood around this small table, which looked as though it was made of wood, but I doubt it, and upon each side of me — apparently out of the very atmosphere itself — appeared two helpers. This time their hoods were drawn back and I could see that each wore a yellow sash and their faces, although smaller, were an exact replica of the face of the taller Being Who stood between the other Two. A perfect "shade" of Himself had been formed, even to the extent that the features were a fine-cut replica of His handsome countenance.

"Before I go, may I ask Your indulgence to answer one more question, please?" I thought.

"Yes, you may write about this and your following experience in this place," was the answer.

I bowed again, filled with the anticipation which would be brought about by the responsibility of having to describe such a majestic meeting as that which had just been experienced in the presence of such Mighty Beings as These.

After this termination of the Holy Meeting, my surroundings quickly vanished and I became suddenly aware of my surroundings — outside on the moor. Dimly, through the darkness and ground fog, I saw the outlines of the Spacecraft in which I had arrived. Immediately I appeared, the panel opened and I felt myself lifted, as if by some invisible force, into the craft and laid down upon a couch.

I remembered no more until my physical eyes opened and I looked around.

I saw a small darkened room, the sunlight just breaking through the curtains across the window which, when my eyes became fully adjusted, I noticed to be red. I was lying beneath a soft covering — on a soft bed which was terrestrial in origin.

I was back again in Santa Barbara.

I rolled over, felt for the black buzzer button and pressed it, and in seconds, my wife and my assistant entered the room and gave me massage for my stiff, aching and, despite the temperature outside, cold limbs. Both of them knew enough not to question me at that time, as after an elevated experience I do not answer questions regarding that experience until I am ready to do so. The time was 1:05 p.m. Pacific Standard Time. So much had happened in one hour and twenty-five minutes that I had to crystallize my thoughts before I was able to do justice to the details of the majestic experience.

Later, I informed both of my helpers that ''Operation Earth Light'' and my modus operandi for its performance, had been accepted by The Lords Of The Flame. I told my wife that, despite appearances to the contrary regarding the health of both of us and the frustrations which had happened in the past week, I wanted this date lodged as the official birthdate of the Mission. My wife wrote up a Directors' Minute covering the official acceptance by The Aetherius Society. I made the proposition, she seconded it. As there were two Directors not present, namely, The Reverend Erain G. Noppe, who was in Los Angeles, and The Reverend Edna Spencer, who was in Detroit, both of these ladies were contacted by telephone and a brief explanation of ''Operation Earth Light'' given to each of them, and their votes were asked for. They gave their votes, making the Directors' votes on the official acceptance of ''Operation Earth Light'' unanimous. Thus, officially and metaphysically, the birthdate of this vital Mission was logged as November 29th, 1979 (Earthyear 16.145).

Once again, I had lived through the almost indescribable honour of an audience with the greatest Beings on this Planet and those Beings had accepted my plans for a Mission which I felt very strongly should be performed. They had, in Their consideration and boundless compassion for me, invited me, yet again, to Their Holy Shrine, but the next time to enjoy even another set of advanced experiences.

I would like to make it known that this experience of the meeting with The Lords Of The Flame is being written in this book only because They gave permission that it could be written.

Even as I write, I feel a deep sense of loss, as though I had given away, without reward, an old and priceless jewel which was a revered heirloom — nay, more than this; as though I had given up a part of my very soul.

An experience such as that I had lived through and witnessed in a superconscious state, was far more real to me than had the same experience been enjoyed in the ordinary physical state of consciousness. I could feel every happening, in this sensitive state, much more acutely, and appreciate its meaning far more vividly, than any conscious mind is capable of. Yet I knew that because The Great Lords had given me permission to describe this outstanding experience, They, for reasons best known to Themselves, and undoubtedly out of compassion for mankind, expected me to do so.

Here are revelations made as ancient as the Planet — yet more modern than tomorrow.

These jewels of wisdom are now enclosed in the pages of a book which will, because of Divine Blessing, become a classic in the metaphysical treatises of the world; for the description of this experience alone, never mind that to follow, must give to all who take it to their hearts, a much deeper appreciation of the magic and unique abilities of The Protectors Of The Ineffable Flame of the Life Force of the Planet upon which we live — The Logos Of Terra.

Yet I must suffer my personal deep loss by revealing these things to you, because The Lords have said so.

I have decided to take no financial gain whatsoever from the sale of the first edition of *Visit To The Logos Of Earth*, but to donate all the profits which are made to The Aetherius Society, for the feeling, deep down in my soul, is that I have received a mystical initiation which is more valuable to me than any monetary consideration.

The Ancient Lords spoke and I have tried my best to obey Them.

I feel that behind Their permission to reveal these ancient truths there is a deeper, more profound reason than either you or I appreciate as yet.

AUTHOR'S RECOMMENDATIONS

NOTE 1. Study the metaphysical lesson available on Cassette No. C-57, *The Devic Kingdom*, for a better understanding of the forces of Nature. It is also recommended that students read The Fifth Blessing, "Blessed Are The Thanksgivers," from the book, *The Twelve Blessings*.

NOTE 2. For information on the continuing Cosmic Mission, "Operation Prayer Power," one of the greatest mass Healing tools ever given to mankind, study of the following cassettes is recommended: Cassette No. C-52, *Operation Prayer Power;* Metacassette® No. MC-12, *Operation Prayer Power — A Spiritual Dream Come True;* and Metacassette® No. MC-13, *Important Declaration Of Truth To Terra.*

Also read *The Aetherius Society Newsletter*, Volume 12, Issues 8-9, May 1973 and Issues 14-17, August 1973; Volume 13, Issues 16-20, August-September 1974; Volume 14, Issue 18, September 1975; Volume 17, Issue 19, August 1978; Volume 18, Issues 23-24, October 1979 and Issues 25-26, October 1979; *Cosmic Voice*, Volume 1, Issues 5-8, October-November 1980; Volume 2, Issues 10-12, August-September 1981; Volume 3, Issues 11-12, November-December 1982; Volume 4, Issues 1-4, January-March 1983; and Volume 5, Issues 5-9, May-July 1984.

For details on how to participate in "Operation Prayer Power," contact your nearest Headquarters of The Aetherius Society, and read the pamphlet, *Operation Prayer Power — A Spiritual Dream Come True*, available free of charge.

NOTE 3. "Operation Starlight" is a Cosmic Mission which was performed by Doctor George King in cooperation with Higher Cosmic Forces, in order that 19 Holy Mountains were Charged with vibrant Spiritual Energies, to be used by ordinary man. For details, read the pamphlet, *The Holy Mountains Of The World*. Also listen to Cassette No. C-27, *Deep Occult Revelations About Operation Starlight* — a must for the advanced student. Read also Chapter 3 of *The Five Temples Of God*, and *Cosmic Voice*, Issues 21-26.

NOTE 4. For information regarding the actions of The Adepts, Who have done so much to protect humanity, read the outstanding book, *The Three Saviours Are Here!*, which gives details of the actions of these Adepts against the lower astral realms of Earth. Also read *The Atomic Mission* and *Destruction Of The Temple Of Death/Rescue In Space*.

NOTE 5. For details of the Cosmic Mission, "Operation Bluewater," study the booklet, *This Is The Hour Of Truth*, and Chapter 4 of the book, *The Five Temples Of God*.

NOTE 6. For information on the effects of radioactivity on the physical and subtle bodies of man, the student is recommended to study Chapter 8 of the book, *You Are Responsible!* which contains information given by The Cosmic Masters regarding this vitally important subject.

NOTE 7. For details of the projected visit made by Doctor George King to the moon in 1956, and of the Space station, read Chapter 3 of *You Are Responsible!* Confirmation of the existence of this Space station was made in 1979 by both American and Soviet scientists. This was reported in the "National Enquirer" of September 11, 1979.

NOTE 8. "Ben Hope" is one of the 19 Holy Mountains Charged in "Operation Starlight." Doctor George King acted as the channel for the initial Charge of Spiritual Energy into this mountain on December 10, 1958. Read the pamphlet, *The Holy Mountains Of The World*, for further details.

Students are also recommended to study the booklet, *My Contact With The Great White Brotherhood*, for information on the occult importance of the Holy Mountains in Scotland.

All the cassettes, books and Newsletters recommended above are currently available from the publishers, The Aetherius Society.

CHAPTER 3

THE LOGOS OF EARTH

In the weeks which followed the outstanding happening on November 29th, 1979 (Earthyear 16.145), I threw myself into work for The Aetherius Society. The main idea was to put together what loose ends I could and these as soon as possible. We started a minor rebuilding programme and complete redecoration of our display area and this resulted, for the first time, in a piece of astrometaphysical equipment which I had designed in 1963 being put on display to the general public. This apparatus was used in the Four Phases of "Operation Bluewater" by Cosmic Intelligences so that Spiritual Energy could be radiated through the apparatus into a Psychic Centre of Earth off the coast of Southern California. According to Cosmic Sources, this release of Spiritual Energy to The Goddess Of Earth, at that exact time, stopped violent underground movements which could have resulted in the flooding of the continental coast from Portland, Oregon, to Ensenada, Mexico. The whole Four Phases of the mighty "Operation Bluewater" were performed between July 11th, 1963, and November 29th, 1964, and to the time of writing, the massive subterranean movements have not taken place, much to the amazement of scientists, who have been studying the precarious position of cities, especially San Francisco. (Note 1.)

I am not claiming that such Earth movements will not take place in the future, but am stating, as you all know, they have not done so over the past 20 years.

For the first time in the history of The Aetherius Society, the machine used was put on display in our little museum and did cause a great deal of interest. After all, it would be logical to assume that anyone living in America should be far more interested in looking at a piece of apparatus through which their country had been helped than the virtually useless art products of an old civilization.

Together with a group of specially chosen Initiates, referred to as "The Operation Sunbeam Task Force," we made a small start on preparing some items for the "Operation Earth Light" equipment. I also prepared and gave a speech to the Society on the accomplishments of 1979 (Earthyear 15/16). So outstanding were these accomplishments that, when they were all put together as rough notes, I was impressed to start this meeting in a different way from any meeting I have yet conducted in my lifetime as a lecturer. (Note 2.)

I feel that in order to educate readers of this book regarding the tremendous value of Spiritual Energy at this turbulent time in the history of mankind on Earth, I should include the statements made in the unusual start of this meeting, together with the two Mental Transmissions I received afterwards in answer to this request.

Statement made at 2:00 p.m., December 30th, 1979 (Earthyear 16.176), at the American Headquarters of The Aetherius Society, at the start of the public meeting on the "Accomplishments Of 1979":

"I am George King, 'Grand Knight Templar Of The Inner Sanctum Of The Holy Order Of The Spiritual Hierarchy Of Earth.' I hereby respectfully request that Mars Sector 8 — Special Advisor S2 adds the data to be given, to His computer banks for the purpose of comparison between these Aetherius Society activities and

No. 1 The Buddhist Religion;

No. 2 The Christian Religion;

in terms of overall help given to mankind in 1979." (Note 3.)

Mental Transmission received at 3:00 p.m., December 30th, 1979 (Earthyear 16.176), during the interval of the same public meeting:

"Your request has been accepted.

"This evaluation will be given shortly.

"Mars Sector 8 — Special Advisor S2."

Then, at 5:22 p.m., January 20th, 1980 (Earthyear 16.197), the following truly shattering answer was received from Cosmic Sources and the requested evaluation was given:

"In answer to your request, the evaluations we are prepared to give now are as follows:

''Operation Sunbeam' and the Spiritual Energy Radiator Availability ('Operation Space Power') was nine hundred and forty-five (945) times more valuable to the physical Realms of life in 1979 than the Buddhist and Christian Religions combined.

''The two Missions were nine thousand, two hundred and thirty-three (9,233) times more valuable in terms of Karmic manipulation, to all Higher Levels, than the Buddhist and Christian Religions together, and eight thousand, five hundred and forty-seven (8,547) times the value of the combined efforts of the Buddhist, Christian, Jewish and Moslem Religions to the Higher Realms.

''Well done — now even the Gods know this.

''Mars Sector 8 — Special Advisor S2.''

Despite all the rest of the valuable work done by The Aetherius Society in 1979, these two Missions alone were hundreds of times more valuable to the physical Realms and thousands of times more valuable to the Higher Realms of life on Earth than a combination of the largest Religions on Earth today. For your information, it is estimated that the Buddhist and Christian Religions together have an estimated one thousand, one hundred and sixty-eight million, one hundred and eighty-four thousand (1,168,184,000) adherents — and the Buddhist, Christian, Jewish and Moslem Religions together have an estimated one thousand, seven hundred and twenty-eight million, five hundred and ninety-two thousand (1,728,592,000) adherents. That a small organization such as The Aetherius Society could be vastly more valuable to all life on the physical and Higher Realms of Earth than these vast numbers of people is readily understandable. It was not the fact that The Aetherius Society Members themselves weighed the Karmic scale so heavily in their favour as the fact that, in ''Operation Sunbeam,'' for instance, Masters from another part of this Galaxy did cooperate in this Mission. Even though I personally designed this Mission — before any other person on Earth — the fact that this Mission was offered to The Logos Of Earth enabled, from a Karmic point of view, Three Cosmic Masters to cooperate with us, and it was They Who sent the amazing sixty-nine thousand (69,000) Prayer Hours of Spiritual Energy through Psychic Centres of this Earth, deep down into the very Logos Itself, during

1979. (Note 4.) This Spiritual Energy, originally meant for the use of mankind, was collected from Holy Mountains around the world and given back to the Earth as a token repayment for the tremendous debt owed to The Logos by mankind throughout his numerous lives on this beautiful sphere of existence. Although I designed the Mission, "Operation Sunbeam," and all the equipment necessary for the correct performance of this Cosmic Mission, I must give the honour of the final success to these Three Great, Enlightened Cosmic Beings.

Mention in the Cosmic Transmission above refers to the "Spiritual Energy Radiator Availability." Since this Cosmic Transmission we have given this Mission a name, and that is, "Operation Space Power." When I originally designed "Operation Sunbeam," I invented equipment which could be used to discharge the Spiritual Energy batteries originally charged by the Three Cosmic Masters from the Star-System, Gotha. Since the big improvement in "Operation Sunbeam," which was initiated on June 14th, 1979 (Earthyear 15.342), this equipment is no longer needed to perform the Mission. Even so, for 14 years, because of its efficient design, this astro-metaphysical apparatus has been used by Cosmic Forces through which to send Spiritual Energies to all Levels of life, not only the physical and above, but even below that, to the lower astral Realms. In 1979 alone, one million, six hundred and seventy-nine thousand, six hundred (1,679,600) Prayer Hours of Spiritual Energy were sent to the physical Realms and the Higher and lower Realms of life connected to the Planet Earth through two Spiritual Energy Radiators, one in America and one in England, which were operated during every Spiritual Push for six hours per day. Once again, I must give the credit for the difference between what The Aetherius Society did and other major Religions in the world, from a Karmic point of view, for all life connected to Earth, through this Mission, "Operation Space Power" — to the Operators of Satellite No. 3, and not myself. (Note 5.) And to repeat for emphasis, these evaluations, given from an unimpeachable Source, above any living on this Earth, do not take into consideration the eight thousand, six hundred and seventy-five (8,675) Prayer Hours we released for world peace in our "Operation Prayer Power" during 1979. Neither do they

THE SPIRITUAL ENERGY RADIATOR

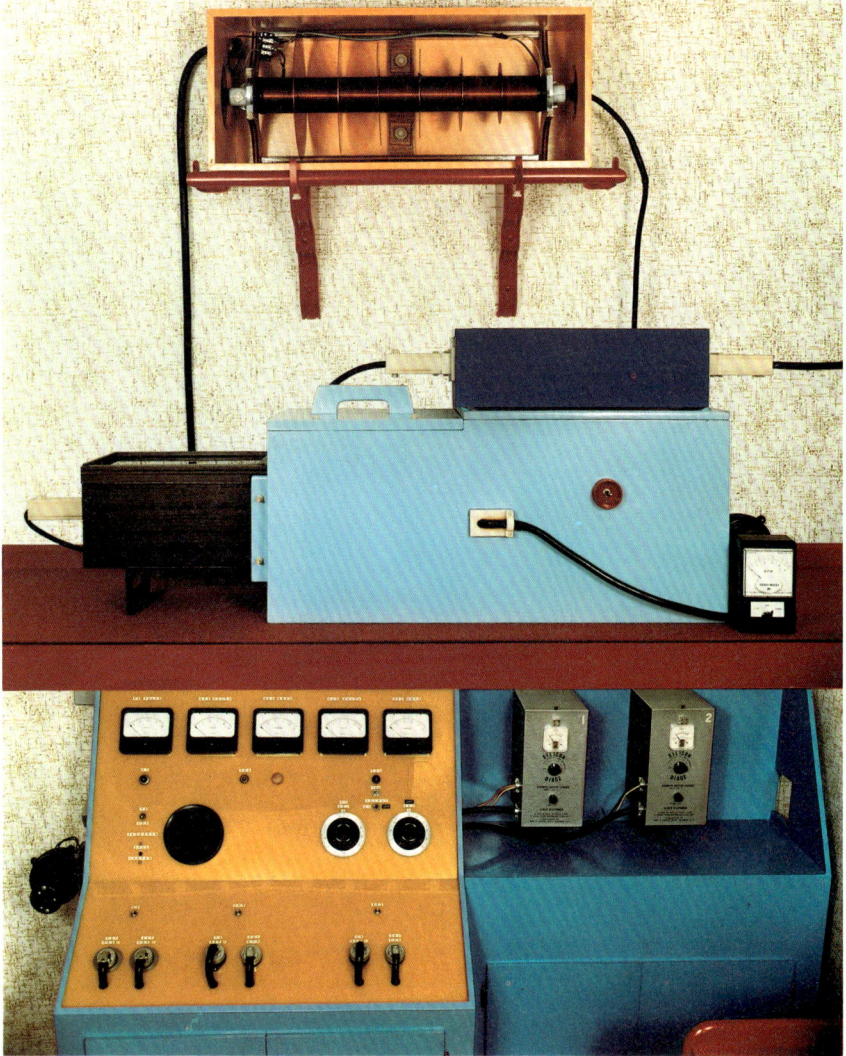

The Spiritual Energy Radiator, designed by Doctor George King and manufactured by the Staff of The Aetherius Society, incorporates advanced concepts of astro-metaphysical science. This remarkable mechanism, used in "Operation Space Power" in conjunction with Satellite No. 3, transmits millions of units of varying frequency Spiritual Energies to all Levels of life on Earth. This versatile machine is also used for the release of Spiritual Energies in "Operation Prayer Power" discharges.

take into consideration the six thousand, five hundred (6,500) Contact Spiritual Healing treatments we gave during that year, or the twenty-three thousand, four hundred (23,400) Absent Healing treatments we gave during that year to people who, because of their illness, had applied to us for help. All these were given free of charge. (Note 6.)

The reasons I am publishing these amazing statistics in this book are twofold: firstly, so that readers can appreciate the stupendous results which can be brought about, for the benefit of the human race, by the manipulation of Spiritual Energies; and secondly, so that readers may better appreciate what a few enlightened people can do for suffering mankind if they use their God-given humanitarian abilities in the correct Spiritual and scientific manner. If they make the initial surrender to God in an *unconditional way*, then modern miracles, such as those detailed by the Cosmic Master, Mars Sector 8 — Special Advisor S2, can be brought about today, even though we live in a world ruled by the golden fist of base materialism.

And all this untold good was done for humanity through a tiny organization which threw its mind, strength and finances into bringing into being specially designed apparatus to help mankind. Although "Operation Space Power" and "Operation Sunbeam" brought about the results which you can see by the Revelations given from Cosmic Sources, both of these Missions had to be performed, because of lack of resources, on a very small scale. Just imagine the stupendous improvements which could be brought into being by the transmission of Spiritual Energies to any part of the world at any time, in any degree and frequency that they were needed, if, for instance, we had had the same backing and support which was thrown into making the first atom bomb to kill the Japanese! Admittedly, the motive for the manufacture of this bomb was firstly to beat the Germans to this invention, then after Germany fell, to shorten the war between the allies and Japan. But, according to official sources, it took one million of the best technicians available, three years to make this bomb and then they only succeeded because of an unlimited budget on which hundreds of millions of dollars were spent! All this effort and finance to make a test bomb and two atom bombs which were dropped on

Hiroshima and Nagasaki — two deadly weapons which killed and maimed thousands of people.

If you knew as much about the mystical science of astro-metaphysics as I do, then you would realize what could be done with the correct use of far less resources than those spent on the first atom bombs. If I had under my direction, several small but well-equipped laboratories, staffed by five or six thousand dedicated technicians who were open-minded enough to study the science of astro-metaphysics, and travel facilities, plus a choice of certain crystals, gold and copper, with a strictly limited budget of less than ten million dollars, the results would be outstanding.

Crops, the like of which have rarely been seen upon Earth, could be grown to feed the masses.

Every operating theatre in every hospital could be equipped with a receiving device which would unerringly pick up specially devised Spiritual Healing Energies to flood the operating theatre during every operation which was performed. The frequencies of these Spiritual Healing Energies could be tuned to the particular requirements of the patient in such a way as to promote the growth of healthy tissues to heal those which had been incised.

Spiritual Energies of the correct frequency could be sent to any trouble spot in the world in order to give those people, genuinely working for peace or rescue in these places, more power and knowledge than they would normally have, thereby enabling their peace missions or rescue services to be more effective than ever before.

Many diseases which, up to the present, have been declared by medical science to be incurable, could be bombarded by a concentration of natural forces and, with adequate experimentation, cures could be found.

This astro-metaphysical science could work hand-in-glove with the orthodox sciences of medicine and diet to eventually, not only make the race much fitter, but also to make people less prone to disease and even accidents.

The dream in the minds of many atomic scientists in the early days was that, despite the terrible weapons they were building, the same technology would be evolved to give to the human race an unlimited supply of energy for all its needs. Half a century later, that dream has not come into manifestation. Atomic power stations in different parts of the world generate some electricity to meet the needs of moving humanity, but as science has found, sometimes to its bitter cost, they do not yet even begin to fill the gap which they are supposed to do because of the inherent dangers and instability within them. What the dreamers of the past and scientists of the present seem to forget and completely leave out of their calculations, was one shining Truth which I, for one, have stated to the public for over 30 years now.

A Truth which will have to be faced sooner or later.

It is simply this, that there is only one energy crisis on Earth at the present time, and that is the Spiritual Energy crisis. Solve this crisis and no other shortages of any kind will exist!

The relatively new, yet most ancient alchemy of astro-metaphysics can solve this Spiritual Energy crisis, providing always that the science is used in the right way for the pure benefit of mankind, by the right people who are dedicated to God. I could write a book on the future of the world if the right minds, technology and financial backing were given to what is now a mysterious science, for the benefit of the human race. And that look into the future would be very different from a visionary's look at our tomorrows.

The astro-metaphysical apparatus I have designed and which has been built by The Aetherius Society, is specifically designed to help mankind in many different ways; in other words, it had the right humanitarian motive directing it. To activate this apparatus in the correct manner needs human beings with the right motive, the right outlook, the right kindness and compassion for suffering humanity. These human beings are, of course, vastly more important than the equipment they operate, which really is just a means to an end. However, human beings being what they are, have imposed such limitations upon themselves that the correct equipment can help them to concentrate and direct their inner forces in a disciplined manner. For instance, instead of reciting selfish Prayers, as do most religious followers upon Earth, we of The Aetherius Society carefully choose the Prayers we use and, with the help of Mantra Teams specially trained to correctly intone ancient Tibetan Mantra, we are able to concentrate the Universal Life Forces, through invocation by Prayer, and store this Spiritual Energy in a physical container in a Mission which we call "Operation Prayer Power." We can then, whenever needed, discharge this Spiritual Energy to any part of the world. It takes approximately 1,200 Prayer Hours to fill one of these Spiritual Energy batteries.

These 1,200 Prayer Hours can be discharged to an area needing relief in approximately 100 minutes! (Note 7.)

If, for instance, a country is hit by an earthquake, the whole area can be flooded with vibrant, uplifting Spiritual Energies invoked by good, devout people who have prayed in the right dynamic fashion. All rescue teams in that area, without even realizing it, will be given greater strength and clarity of thought so that they can perform their rescue services better than ever before. Imagine if that one Mission was performed on a worldwide scale, what a colossal difference this would make to your life in the present, and your children's life in the future!

There is no doubt in the mind of any open-minded, honest researcher that Spiritual Healing does work. The Christian Religion was founded by a great Spiritual Healer — not one Who had unique God-given gifts above those given to everybody, but one Who used His inner abilities for the benefit of mankind and that was the secret of the success of the person you call Jesus of Nazareth! Just imagine if modules, placed in every hospital in the world, were activated by Prayer Teams numbering only ten million carefully trained and devout people, what Healing could be unerringly directed to these hospitals. Even if you know only a little about Spiritual Healing, then you can see immediately the stupendous good which could be brought about by the use of this aspect of a brave new science by a brave new world.

There is one thing for sure that, if you, as an aspect of God and a member of the human race, demonstrated your inner abilities and compassion to help in such a project, your conscience would be a clear one.

What a comparison — a million specially chosen, highly skilled people working for three years with an unlimited budget to make an atom bomb to kill, and a small organization like The Aetherius Society devoting most of its extremely limited resources to perform several Missions designed to help the Karma of mankind. Little wonder, is it not, that our efforts, strictly disciplined and directed as they were, backed up by great personal sacrifice, were proved to be more effective than those of the huge religious masses.

But then, application of the deeper knowledge within brings about the miracles.

Some time ago, while in contemplation, I received this Truth which I feel is the answer to all of our problems:

''I am naught,'' said a man. ''Naught but Me,'' answered God.

Despite the fact that, being in a human body, I was thrilled to my very soul by the fact that we, as a small, active organization, had been given the privilege and opportunity of helping mankind in the way that we were in 1979, I was always remembering the further invitation by The Lords Of The Ineffable Flame Of The Logos Of Earth to re-visit Them and to learn more of The Logos Herself. Although my ''Operation Earth Light'' had been accepted by The Great Lords on November 29th (Earthyear 16.145), I still felt a promise of other Revelations to come and may say that I awaited expectantly for Their further Holy invitation. Oh yes, I did this with some trepidation, for whosoever has been in such a Sacred Presence before, although loving every minute of that Presence, must, if they have any deep appreciation at all, feel very small in such a Holy Presence. This law certainly applied to me. No matter what you have done for the world and, judging by indisputable Cosmic Intelligence, I had been responsible for doing a tremendous amount of good, even so, in a Presence like that of The Lords Of The Flame, one's importance dwindles to nothingness.

If the search for Truth is your greatest ambition, and it should be, your search will be doomed to failure unless you are truthful in your dealings with others as well as yourself. This is one of the great occult secrets of life but one seldom realized by the student. You cannot understand that which is outside of yourself unless a part of that is lodged most firmly within. I am but a simple man with a great yearning to learn the secrets of Truth. In my varied life I have learned that the surest step upon the ladder to real success — not that passing state which a materialist calls success — but lasting success, is to **surrender oneself unconditionally to God** and throw the whole of your efforts into helping mankind to do the same thing. And to perform this most sacred of all practices in the right way, one must be prepared even to reveal the cherished happenings of their greatest hours. Although, when such Revelation is made, one feels a far more acute sense of loss than any material loss can bring about, however, you also feel something else which makes up for this, an inner contentment that at least you have helped others along the road which you have found to be successful and enlightening.

A little over two weeks after the lecture to The Aetherius Society which gave a concise report of our accomplishments in the vitally important year 1979, I had the honour of receiving another Mental Transmission which I had awaited with great expectations. This Mental Transmission was delivered to me by The Lord Babaji Himself, Who is the Spiritual Head of The Spiritual Hierarchy Of Earth, at 5:15 p.m. on January 20th, 1980 (Earthyear 16.197).

"It is my pleasure to extend to you a further invitation from The Protectors Of The Ineffable Flame Of The Logos Of Terra on January 23rd, 1980 (Earthyear 16.200) at 2:00 p.m. your time.
"Have an enlightened day on that which you call your birthday.
    "Babaji."

Like all really great men, The Lord Babaji has a way of imparting information in an honest, straightforward manner. This Transmission, although short and to the point, meant a great deal to me, as you all can realize. The promised return invitation by The Lords Of The Flame had now been delivered and what is more, the meeting was to take place on my 61st birthday.

Although not feeling that I deserved the honour of receiving a birthday present of such magnitude as this, I nevertheless prepared for the coming event. It is a certain fact that the more active you are, if you have to leave that activity suddenly, the more loose ends you have to tie together before you can safely leave, and this happened to me. However, after some hard work and planning necessary to keep the Society actively engaged in the right direction, I left Los Angeles with my wife on January 22nd, 1980 (Earthyear 16.199), and arrived in Santa Barbara in the early afternoon.

The weather was absolutely gorgeous, the Sun shining beautifully with daytime temperatures in the low 70°'s, and night-time temperatures in the low 40°'s. Even though we had heavy rains for

days before this, the weather had cleared almost as though to wel-
come me to the next stage of my enchanting journey into Wisdom.
Despite the heavy workload my wife and I had assigned ourselves
over the past three weeks, we both felt better in health this time
than we did previously.

After spending a relaxing, pleasant evening on January 22nd, I
began preparations for the visit to The Holy Lords. The oxygen
breathing equipment was tested in the same way that it was prior
to my previous visit on November 29th. The buzzer system
was set up again as both my wife and assistant would be sitting
quietly in the living room down the hallway, while I would lie on
the bed as I had done during the previous visit.

After pulling the curtains I settled myself down on the bed so
that my spine was straight — so important to astral projection — at
1:40 p.m. on January 23rd, 1980 (Earthyear 16.200). At 1:45 p.m.
I started my deep breathing exercises and Mantra in earnest. This
time the air, charged by negative ions caused by the reaction of
sunlight impregnating the lawns and vegetation outside, seemed
to be a more definite help than before, or maybe I was more aware
of this than I had been previously. However, every breath I took
seemed to bring life and confidence to me and, as far as the latter
was concerned, I needed whatever help I could get. I had been
promised this time, by The Great Lords, that more information regarding The Logos Herself would be given to me. That was indeed a great promise which meant far more than I can tell you.
However — and I could not help being worried about this during
my preparations — a much greater responsibility rested upon my
shoulders because of this. In fact, that thought seemed most prevalent in my mind this time. Even so, freedom from the human
body seemed to be a lot easier and the division was made more
quickly and without the mental exertion which had to be used on
November 29th. No sooner had I started my deep breathing and
the mental manipulations which enhanced it, as well as thinking
about a very Holy Mantra, freedom seemed to come to me and, in
a very short time, I was able to look down at my aging physical
body lying in deep trance in my little bedroom in Santa Barbara.

No sooner had the projected release been brought about than I
was again received by The Adepts in one of Their Spacecraft. It

was the same vehicle as before but Three of Them only were present: The Master Babaji, together with ''Nixies Zero Zero Four'' and ''Nixies Zero Zero Five.'' These latter Two Adepts do not live in a gross physical structure as we on Earth do, but have taken on a subtle body and They live on any plane on Earth where They can be of the most use to mankind in Their Cosmic Mission to this Planet.

The Master Babaji Himself came forward and after making a certain hand sign, congratulated me on the accomplishments of last year! I telepathed some adequate reply in answer to His congratulations, but whatever it was, probably did not express the honour which was felt having been congratulated by the greatest Master in The Spiritual Hierarchy of this Planet. A Being Who has lived in a terrestrial body on Earth throughout countless centuries and One Who has promised that He will not leave Earth until mankind no longer needs His guidance, provides a great honour to all who have had the privilege of a personal meeting with Him. Even though there is an uncommon bond of brotherly love existing between myself and The Lord Babaji, I am always aware of a much more Holy Presence than my own whenever I have the pleasure of being in His company.

After the greeting, I was informed by Adept ''Nixies Zero Zero Four'' to clothe myself in a certain type of uniform. This was not made of the same material as that I had donned previously but was light blue in colour and was very much thicker, although almost as resilient as that worn previously. I was told that this was an essential garment which would offer protection for me during the Initiation which was to follow.

One thing about the uniform which was entirely different was the fact that — and I thank Them for it — the Crest of my station, that of a ''Grand Knight Templar Of The Inner Sanctum Of The Holy Order Of The Spiritual Hierarchy Of Earth,'' was embossed across the front of this uniform. And a magnificent emblem it was too. I was asked to stand in front of what obviously was an electronic camera and on a screen, in full colour, I could see myself and also see details of this magnificent Coat Of Arms. (Note 8.)

Against a dark red background, covered with mystical symbols in a bright gold colour, was a clenched hand and an arm to the el-

GREAT WHITE BROTHERHOOD CREST

A simplified version of the Crest as worn in action by ''The Grand Knights Templar Of The Inner Sanctum Of The Holy Order Of The Spiritual Hierarchy Of Earth.'' In the original, the dark red background is covered by a complex pattern of mystical symbols. However, the illustration conveys to the reader an authentic idea of the mystical symbology of this powerful Crest.

bow. Around the arm was curled a magenta-coloured snake which rose up so that it was gripped firmly by the clenched hand and protruded above the fist. But this magenta-coloured snake did not end in a snake's head, but a multi-coloured star which threw its rays across the background of the Coat Of Arms. As I looked at it I was told the meaning, even though it seemed fairly obvious to me, of the symbology depicted in this Crest:

"The snake is the universal representation for the power of Kundalini and you will see that this power is controlled exactly and runs through the fist to end in a torch from which Spiritual Energies are given to the world.

"You will notice that there are no jewels or no metal in this Crest as it is a combat replica of its original counterpart which contains several different metals and many jewels."

These thoughts were relayed to me by one of The Adepts, known only to man as "Nixies Zero Zero Four." I could see immediately the danger of using metals and specially jewels, which may be susceptible to the reception of all energies, good or bad, in a combat replica of this Crest. Immediately I thought about this, these thoughts were confirmed by The Adept.

"It would appear that you know something about the type of combat to which I referred," was the telepathic rejoinder which "Nixies Zero Zero Four" made, with a slight smile puckering the corners of His lips.

"Books, you know — I have read books," I thought quickly.

"Oh yes, books — that's right, there must be many books published on Earth describing lower astral combat sessions," chided the Other.

We all laughed at that.

After that the conversation became serious for The Master Babaji came forward and discussed certain things with me which I will not publish at this time. While all this was going on, without me being aware of the motion of the craft, we had taken off and were proceeding towards our objective.

"As you will be having an experience different from that you had previously, you will enter through the North Polar entrance," stated Babaji.

And in answer to my thought of alarm, for I knew the North

Polar entrance to be one of extreme danger, He informed me that special provision had been made by the installation of a modification to that entrance which had been made quite recently.

I knew there were four main entrances into the inner core of Earth, the domicile of The Great Lords, but the North and South Polar entrances necessitated a long journey being made around half the inside of the world, to avoid being trapped by the surging streams of "element X," which were extremely active beneath the outer core. That the safest entrance, for a neophyte like myself, even in a projected form with specially designed protective clothing, was the one in England I had used last time.

Soon we came over the North Polar region — I will not, at this stage, say whether this was the True North or the Magnetic North, for reasons of security — however, we came into our position and beneath me I could see the massive ice-covered crags of the Polar region. I do not feel that I would have been able to see them through the darkness and thick clouds, even through psychic eyes, but using specialized equipment on board the Spacecraft I could see them projected in colour on one of the internal vision screens.

"We will vibrate onto a Higher Level from where the entrance will be made," stated The Master Babaji. "And you will then appreciate the modifications of which I spoke."

Suddenly the Earth disappeared from the screen which was now covered with flashes of blue, green, yellow and black, like great pointed fingers which travelled from one side of the screen to the other and we were above a very different landscape in the matter of seconds. I could now see plainly through one of the portholes of the craft, which gave an undistorted view of the landscape beneath. It was a different type of landscape from that on the physical Realms of Earth, even though it did represent the North Polar region on this Higher Realm. This is not an excuse by any means, but I will not describe that landscape, as to do so could be a breach of important security.

Looking through the porthole intently, with an enhanced vision which is a part of projection, I could see a thin, slender, pale green tube which emanated from out of the ground beneath and rose hundreds of feet into the air.

"It will be necessary for you to move into this special capsule and you will be launched into that tube where a Reception Committee will await you on entrance to the Inner Chambers,'' thought Babaji so clearly that I could understand every word that He telepathed to me.

I took one more look at the screen, while standing in front of the camera, at my dress in this light blue resilient but not shiny material and was very glad, for my own confidence sake, that I carried the Crest over my chest. This was not the only insignia I wore. At least, if nothing else, I was dressed for the part, I thought, to the amusement of the Others in the Spacecraft.

I entered the canister, which was standing upright on the floor, and before the panel was closed, I tested my breathing apparatus and temperature control which were on the outside of the suit, rather the same as those on the first suit I wore, only these were larger and the controls were more easily accessible and built in a much more rugged way than those on what I took to be the lighter type of clothing worn previously. Again, there were no seams in this protective clothing which enclosed me completely from the ankles to the neck which ended in a metallic-looking — though it was not metal — band upon which fastened the helmet quickly and positively. I wore boots made of the same type of material which came up above the ankles and were sealed to the trousers in a positive manner. In fact, while they were being put on they were pressure tested to make sure that there was no leakage either from the outside or from the inside of the pressurized suit.

The canister was about seven feet high and large enough for me to stand in upright and even move around in at first. When the panel was closed in front of me I felt gentle pressure on parts of the body and discovered that I seemed to be held easily, but at the same time, firmly in this oval canister, the body of which was round. I felt that this was not made of a metal substance and if it was, then I have not seen a metal like it on Earth, because it gave the impression of being immensely strong and yet not hard as metal would be.

Exactly what happened then I am not sure, although I did have vision ahead of me through what I must describe as a porthole. The canister was moved — and not by The Adepts pushing it, either — towards one side of the craft where I had the impression it was locked into even a larger tube and then I had nothing to do but wait. I prepared myself for a shock which could be caused by some release forces, air pressure, or something like that, but no shock came and, to be really honest with you, I did not feel any difference whatsoever as far as motion was concerned when the canister was released. In fact, I could not have told you when this canister, or projectile, was released from the Spacecraft, but became aware of the normal sights being changed outside my port-hole when it became covered with a pale green luminescence. This soon turned slightly darker, when I must have entered the crust of the Earth itself. All the way down this tube, I could only see the iridescence of the magnetic tube down which I travelled and did not, as I had during the last visit, become aware of the different layers of the Earth through which I passed. It was rather like going down in an enclosed lift, with a pale green phosphorescent light outside, except that I did not feel the motion of descent; in fact, I felt no motion whatsoever on this descent. How this was done was "mysterious" but nevertheless absolutely true.

How long I travelled in this manner I do not know, or what distance was covered, I did not, at the time, have any realization. Bear in mind, entering the subtle tube from a higher vibrational frequency than the physical Realms of Earth and travelling through this magnetic tube, brought my existence into another time-frame sequence, quite different from that which we know on the base physical Realms. I remember, at the time, being at first quite surprised at the fact that, in order to make this entrance correctly, it was necessary to vibrate up onto a Higher Realm, but then, after a moment's thought, I could see the reason behind it all. One of strictest possible security. While life on the Higher Realms of Earth is Spiritually advanced, that on the lower Realms of Earth is not Spiritually advanced but very scientifically advanced. Therefore, in order to protect Their entrance, The Lords had foreseen the possibility of intrusion, hence the somewhat elaborate precautions which They had taken.

I would like to state here that I would not envy any entity, be it a powerful evil magician from the lower Realms, or even an alien life form who had discovered this entrance and tried to travel through it without permission. I feel such intelligences would seal their own fate by such an attempt. However, it dawned on me that The Great Lords undoubtedly felt that the prevention of a confrontation was better than the action which They would need to take during such a confrontation. Even though anyone possessing Their powers of telekinesis would be more than capable of protecting Themselves, or indeed, any other entity who They had volunteered to protect, hence Their most ancient title, "Protectors Of The Flame."

Although the journey had been, as far as I was concerned, motionless, I could not help preparing myself for the eventual end of this journey. The canister had to stop sometime and within the confines of the container, I automatically prepared myself for a bump when it did stop. Although there was no scenery moving past the window of the canister to give me a point of reference as to my velocity, I did feel that I was travelling at a considerable speed. Movement inside the canister was very difficult because there was some magnetic device holding me in a certain position, no doubt for my own safety. All the more reason why I should prepare for the bump when it came.

Eventually it did come.

Though it was not the kind of jarring experience which I was prepared for, but a very light touch, not only confined to my feet and legs, but as though the whole body, in some strange way, took the very gentle shock and therefore, it was hardly perceptible. It was a very strange experience — going to a Higher Realm, being launched through a subtle, pale green tube which one knows leads into the bowels of the very Planet Itself, feeling no motion, not being able to take any point of reference on changing scenery outside — for the only thing I could see was the iridescence of the pale green tube — and then stopping with the slightest touch, was, in itself, a very strange, other-worldly experience. Here was a science in application, the secrets of which were not known to terrestrial life forms.

The slight touch told me that the descent of the canister had ceased and I felt the magnetic pull exerted on the outside of my body, through the garment, released. Without me having to make any move, the canister slid open and I stepped out. It took me a short time to become aware of my surroundings.

The first thing I saw was the same type of light globules which I had seen during my previous visit. These were hovering above my head, a long way above my head, and again, they illuminated the cave-like room in which I stood without appearing themselves to be excessively bright.

Immediately, two Beings materialized in front of me and each of them was dressed in the dark, robe-like garment with hoods covering their faces entirely, but I noted that each of these wore a yellow sash around the middle. They were "shades" made by One of The Great Lords and had been programmed to act as what could be described as a Reception Committee.

"Come."

The word, perfectly telepathed, came into my mind in a much clearer way than had I heard it through my normal ears. I followed the two "shades," for immediately after giving the telepathic instructions, they turned their backs on me and started to walk, quite quickly, across the stone surface of the huge room, or cave, in which I found myself. Again, this was completely devoid of all furnishings and decorations, except for the several hundred globes of light which floated high overhead. I could not help looking back as I hurried to keep up with my two guides and saw the globes, as though affected by some strange magnetic attraction, begin to follow. They did not come down any lower than they were when I first saw them, but they moved across the space 50 or 60 feet above me and came into a cluster and followed in a silent, unerring, almost weird manner.

After walking on the ground for a few yards, I, like the others ahead, left the ground and began to float, and although again it was difficult to lock onto a point of reference, however, I had the feeling that we were proceeding at a considerable pace. After travelling like this for what may have been a few minutes, I felt myself sink down to the ground again and lightly touched the rocky ground with the balls of my feet. Although I had not thought the projection into being, nevertheless, it was as though the "shades," acting as my guides, had levitated me so that we could travel more quickly than if we had walked in the normal fashion. No sooner had we alighted on the ground than I was instructed that it was safe to remove my helmet. This I did and grasped it with the left hand and stood waiting in all expectancy to see what would happen next. Even though I was in a projected body, which is far more adaptable and advanced than the physical structure, I still felt my heart centre throbbing with a mixture of expectancy and trepidation. I felt like an absolute stranger who had no right to be there. However, hardly had this thought begun to undermine my self-confidence than The Three Great Beings materialized in front of me.

They did not walk up to me — but suddenly appeared!

As if to set my mind at rest, One of Them approached me, holding out both of His hands in front of Him with the palms facing me, and His words lodged themselves in my mind:

"We congratulate you on your recent achievements."

After He had stated these words, picture after picture appeared in my mind illustrating the reasons for His congratulations. I saw quite clearly, flashing segments of our "Operation Prayer Power." People in different parts of the world were reciting Mantra and praying with their hearts and souls in front of our small battery. I saw that battery put onto the discharge apparatus and great waves of Spiritual Energy sweeping, from the antenna, across the surface of Earth to suffering peoples in all places. I saw three Spacecraft manipulating that energy on behalf of Cambodia. Then the mental pictures changed abruptly to our "Operation Sunbeam" Mission through which last year alone, The Masters from the Star-System called Gotha had released the equivalent of sixty-nine thousand (69,000) Prayer Hours of Spiritual Energy to The Logos Of Earth as a token repayment for what She had done for mankind throughout the centuries. I saw this Spiritual Energy leap forward in massive blue — green — red — silver and gold flashes, down through two of the Psychic Centres of The Logos. But the greatest picture of all I was then given was of happenings in two small rooms, one in Los Angeles, and an even tinier one in London, where gigantic beams of vibrant Spiritual Energy leapt across Space from that majestic Third Satellite, one thousand five hundred and fifty (1,550) miles above the surface of Earth, through two machines and out to those people ready to use these uplifting, most magnificent Spiritual Energies. (Note 9.)

After this wondrous picturization, which took place in my mind in seconds, came other picturizations, some of them not so pleasant, all depicting happenings which had taken place during the past year. I was mentally taken to the lower hells and saw two men in desperate hand-to-hand combat and it became obvious that one of them was trying to stop the other from igniting a powerful bomb in the basement of a large building. That he did stop the ignition of this bomb is definitely to his credit, for thousands would have been annihilated in a flash had he not been able to do this.

I felt a stab of pain — excruciating pain, and then it left me as quickly as it had appeared.

I saw an alien probe of non-human entities on Earth, a lightning-like exchange between them and The Adepts, and their alien mission aborted as they raced away through Space.

These pictures came and went as The Lords saw fit without my comment or control. This struck me as the most effective way possible of conveying one's congratulations to another, to be able to show him, in a few fleeting moments, as to what those congratulations refer and why he should deserve them.

The mental pictures ended as abruptly as they had started.

"But enough of this — come."

The Three of Them turned and walked across the floor and I followed, together with the two yellow-sashed "shades." I tried very hard to control my thoughts in the presence of these Great Beings, knowing Them to be telepaths of the most advanced nature. The struggle within me must have been noted because into my mind floated the command:

"Do not worry, we realize this."

I swallowed hard and worried all the more after this statement!

Just put yourself in my position for a moment. Here I was in the presence of the greatest Beings on the Planet Who knew my every mood, my every movement, my every thought, and none of these moods, movements or thoughts could be kept from Them — how would you feel? You are right — I felt the same!

Although I realized that I was not the first person who had come to this Holy place and had come into contact with The Great Lords Of The Flame, however, I knew that such meetings were, to say the least, extremely rare, and despite the fact I carried credentials which were themselves extremely rare, I still could not allow my full confidence to take control of me.

Two things bring confidence: one, ignorance; the other, great Wisdom. Ignorance will bring confidence because it knows no better; Wisdom will bring confidence because it does know why. However, in Company such as this, I felt anything but knowledgeable.

As we walked, the globes followed, in methodical fashion, way above our heads and threw illumination around this huge place. I still did not see any furnishings but did see that the floor upon which we walked had changed from what looked like a flat grey rock to what now appeared rather like marble, though not polished as is the marble used on the surface for gravestones or carvings. This was light in colour, with the vein markings in it and seemed to be very flat, as though it were a huge marble deposit which had been flattened by some means unknown to me, but not reflecting as much light as would polished marble.

The Three Beings, wearing magenta robes without any ornamentation or decoration that I could see, stopped in front of me and naturally, I pulled up behind Them. I still had not seen the ceiling of this huge, barn-like room, if room it was, neither had I seen the walls, even though the globes had lighted the place very well. So gigantic was it that I could not tell its size because no point of reference was visible upon which to make my calculations. It just dawned on me then, to be lost in this huge cavern, without light, would indeed be a most terrifying experience.

I looked ahead past The Three Lords and, for the first time, saw what I took to be a massive door in front of us. They beckoned me to come forward, which I did, and in the light of the moving spheres above, I could see that it was indeed a massive door but not made of wood or any material I could recognize. One of the Beings, the tallest One, Who, rightly or wrongly, I took to be the Chief Lord Of The Flame, made a movement in the air with His two hands and, without a sound, this massive portal — the size of which I have no conception for I could not see the top of it then

— moved downwards then inwards, and we stepped down and entered a much smaller room. I looked back, in the natural reaction of a surface-dweller, and saw the gigantic portal slide slowly but silently upwards out of the floor and then close outwards behind me, moving a section of the floor with it as it did so.

Now, the room which we entered was large but not near the proportions of the room, or cave, outside. For the first time, I could see the walls and the ceiling and noted that this was a large structure, about the size of a concert auditorium, or so it seemed. When my eyes focused on the domed walls, I noticed that the auditorium was circular, with a domed ceiling. There were tapestries hanging over the walls. I could not, at first, make them out until requested to walk across the room and examine them. I first started off in one direction, which was corrected by a thought impulse — not my own — and was steered into another direction.

I seemed to cover that large domed Hall in no time at all and appeared before a collection of draperies upon which were embroidered, or fashioned, the Crests of the famous. I saw the ceremonial Crest of The Spiritual Hierarchy Of Earth, together with the different ceremonial Coats Of Arms representing each of the major Retreats around this world. More by feeling than pure impulse, I moved to one side, slowly looking at these famous insignias, and then suddenly came to an abrupt halt in front of one of them which was a much larger replica of the Coat Of Arms I wore on my suit. But this was not made of plastic material as the one on my uniform was, but, like the others there, was studded with jewels and was embroidered in what appeared to be pure gold thread of some thickness. I looked below the Crest of ''The Grand Knights Templar Of The Inner Sanctum Of The Holy Order Of The Spiritual Hierarchy Of Earth'' and saw some names which were carved on crystal slabs inlaid with gold which glistened in the light. One of the names I recognized immediately.

It was my own.

There were several more names there as well which I also recognized, but for security reasons, will not reveal — at this time — the identities of the Grand Knights Templar.

I became aware of a Presence behind me and looked around

and saw The Tall Lord standing there with a slight smile on His passive countenance.

"This is not only our Hall Of Records but also Remembrance," He telepathed to me.

"Every person who has ever lived upon the surface of this Planet and who has either been Initiated into The Spiritual Hierarchy Of Terra, or has performed some outstanding Service for mankind, is recognized beneath his Crest, if he has one, or his name only. We do not need computer systems to remember the deeds connected to every name in this place."

I looked around this large dome-shaped Hall and there must have been hundreds of tapestries and thousands of names adorning those walls. Some of them had been there for thousands of years: Buddha, Jesus, Krishna, Patanjali — all the great names were there throughout the centuries, and I was struck with deep admiration and awe in what was almost a living Presence of these Great Beings Who had come to this Planet, throughout the ages, to help mankind in his progress through Evolution. Had the experience ended there, I would have received more enlightenment than I deserved. I would like to have stayed there for hours, not as an antiquarian, but to be in the presence of such beauty and majesty as that depicted on those magnificent tapestries and on the crystal slabs would have been more than sufficient reward for anything that I had ever done.

My reminiscences were disturbed by The Three Lords, Who this time came and stood around me and each extended Their hands outwards and upwards and the whole scene abruptly changed and I found myself, together with The Lords, in even another Chamber.

"This is our Inner Sanctuary Of Records. The names contained herein, some of which are duplications of the names in the Great Hall, are Those Who have performed the noblest deeds of all. You can recognize that, can you not?"

He pointed to a tapestry hanging upon the wall which contained the names and true identities of The Six Adepts, together with Their true birthplaces!

Beneath these names, carved in hieroglyphics on three massive stone slabs, was a brief history of what The Adepts had done for mankind on Earth. I could not understand the hieroglyphics at first, but even as I looked at the first few sentences, the translation came automatically into my mind. A brief description of the eviction of the alien; the part played by The Adepts in "The Initiation Of Earth"; "Operation Karmalight," and other Missions, were described in brief but beautiful words on those everlasting tablets of honour, paying respect to these Six Great Beings. As I moved slowly away, I could see other names, other descriptions. Becoming more aware of my overall surroundings, I saw that the walls contained many scrolls of honour to those Who had performed deeds which were above the deeds expected either by a terrestrial or Interplanetary Intelligence for a more backward race of individuals.

This was the Hall Of Superb Merit.

Despite the control I tried to exercise over my emotions, even though far more controlled in a projected state than in the physical body, I did shed tears of sheer gladness for what I had seen in this most glorious Inner Sanctuary Of Records.

"We also have another Hall, which contains the names and histories of an entirely different set of individuals — what you may call the 'arch-criminals,' but we have not time to visit that place now. Come."

I followed behind, dazed with the wonderful experience I had just lived through, and the fact that The Lords had seen fit to give it to me. The Three of Them stopped and a similar occurrence took place as happened previously, namely, a table seemed to materialize out of the very air in front of us, and on that table was a tall, fluted crystal glass containing some amber-coloured liquid.

"Drink that. It will not only prepare you better for what you are now about to experience, but when you arrive back in your physical body, the nervous reaction will be more bearable."

I reached out with my right hand and hesitated for a moment, then I peeled off the heavy glove encasing it. I then took hold of the glass and drank the contents in two or three gulps. The amber liquid tasted slightly sweetish; although I do not know what it was made of, it was extremely smooth and I could swallow it quite easily. It tasted rather like — only not quite the same as — a good rosé wine, except a little sweeter. There was no burning sensation as there would be with a hard alcoholic drink and I felt that it was not alcoholic or a drug, but probably a collection of vitamins, combined in a certain way in order to bring about a predetermined result. My head cleared and my eyesight seemed to improve after taking this specially prepared draught. No sooner had I set the crystal goblet down upon the table than the table and goblet just disappeared in front of my very eyes, leaving only a vacant space where they had been just moments before.

In Their compassion for me, The Lords waited for a short time and then a thought came strongly into my mind as They directed it.

"It was your expressed desire to learn more of The Logos Of Earth. Our mental promptings will not teach you as much as one look at a small part of this Cosmic Phenomenon. Know you that no one, in your position, has ever seen The Logos of a Planet in Its Total Expression and ever lived to speak of it. However, a vision of this will be given to you, in part, so that you may have some small comprehension of the greatness of the Total Expression."

After that, the taller of The Lords turned away and another One approached me and directed me to replace my helmet which had been grasped in my left hand until this time. I replaced the helmet without any fumbling and the glove over my right hand. The Lord carefully scrutinized the whole uniform with an Eye which looked past the uniform and into my very etheric structure. He seemed quite satisfied with what He saw and turned with the Others and walked away from me.

I followed.

At this time there were only the four of us in this Inner Hall Of Merit; the "shades" who had been in attendance off and on, were nowhere to be seen. As soon as we started to walk across the floor, a beam of green light appeared in front of me and each of The Lords in turn stepped into it and disappeared before my very eyes.

They must have known that I would do the same and, again out of kindness, They did not treat me as a child, but as a grown, intelligent person. Without a moment's hesitation, I stepped into this circle of green light and to anyone watching, I would, too, have disappeared from their view. I did not feel any extraordinary sensation, save a slight prickling on the outside of my body, despite the heavy protective garment, which must have lasted for one or two seconds and then it was over, and I was standing in one of the strangest Temples — I do not know what else to call it — which I have ever seen.

I have had a very varied experience and have lived through many strange happenings in my 67 years of inhabitation of my present body. I have even projected to other worlds and have seen one or two of the Temples there, as also have I seen in detail the massive Temple Of Worship on Level Four. (Note 10.) But I have never, ever seen anything quite like the place I was in then. I do not really quite know how to describe it and the reader must bear with me for what must be a very inadequate description of a place so great and so Holy that even at first sight I was awed by it.

We were in a very huge room, or cavern — maybe that is the right word for it. Thousands of globes of pinkish light hung at different levels above me. Even though the room was illuminated, I still did not see the ceiling as it seemed to disappear into a dark abyss, high above my head. On the far side of this massive cavern there was a structure. It seemed to be a full mile away from where I stood, but as we moved, we seemed to cover the distance at an amazing speed considering we were not levitating this time, but actually walking across an unpolished but flat crystalline floor. Unlike the marble I had seen previously, this floor was constructed of a crystalline rock which gave off a dull cream reflection in the pinkish glow coming from above. This flat rock floor did not have any noticeable veins of darker material which can be seen in marble. When about 400 yards from the structure at the end, The Three Lords stopped and I pulled up sharply behind Them.

"You will hear tumultuous sound; however, your helmet will protect you," were the words which floated into my mind.

I then became aware that we had all stopped before a magnetic screen which you could see through without distortion, but could not pass through until it had been taken down. I may say, until this time there was a silence which I have never "heard" before, only on very rare occasions on the surface of Earth. The air was so still — naturally, of course, my protective suit seemed to make it that way — but I felt that outside there was complete and absolute stillness, and if this is possible, complete and absolute silence.

It was only when I moved near to the screen that I became aware of it. Aware is a better term than could see it, although, standing near to this screen and looking upwards, I could see that the globules of light, which had followed us, had stopped at a certain distance from the screen. I could also notice a thin bluish iridescence which I could only see when near to the screen and looking up towards the ceiling. With eyes straight ahead you would not even notice a screen was there unless you had an advanced awareness.

"*You will now activate all systems within your protective clothing,*" came the instruction.

I had been taught previously how to do this and followed The Lord's instruction without any hesitation. The temperature in the suit immediately changed and started to drop quickly. I felt the air change as it was impregnated with an above-normal negative ion charge. Although, as stated previously, it is possible to exist for a time without breathing when in a projected state, however, if breathing is possible, it makes existence less complicated as one does not have to concentrate on the intake of Universal Life Forces through certain psychic centres in the subtle body. This suit was specially equipped for life support in environments which would be considered alien to a terrestrial life form. Very shortly I was to offer a Prayer of thanks to the brilliant science which had been expended in order to make such a garment.

After obeying instructions, I looked at The Three Lords Who, by the way, were still dressed in Their simple, shining magenta robes with no protection whatsoever over Their heads. One of Them, Whom I took to be the Leader, moved His arm through the air in a half circle and the screen must have been instantly taken down for it was then I became aware of the "tumultuous sound." It was as though a stormy sea was crashing on hard unyielding rocks with a deep rumble which seemed to ebb and flow like mighty waves. And yet, at the same time, the sound held a definite rhythmic quality which I find difficult to describe.

But what really amazed me was the Light.

An intense, almost blinding Light came from atop the structure a few hundred yards ahead of us. The screen must have had the ability, not only to deaden the sound, but also to filter out certain frequencies of this Light. I felt One of The Lords tap my helmet twice and a darkened visor, which I had not activated, slipped down in front of my face. After that, the Light, although tremendously intense, was more bearable.

"A small aspect of The Planetary Logos Of Terra."

The words floated into my somewhat dazed mind as One of The Lords, with a gesture of His hand, invited me to go forward. I did so, almost hypnotized by the blinding Light ahead of me, until I came to what I have termed, "the structure." It was rather like steps leading up to an Altar, but an Altar with a difference. The steps were huge in comparison with any cathedral steps I have ever seen — they must have been 200 or 300 yards long and, at a guess, 50 yards wide. They were made of the same type of crystalline substance as the floor, at least some of them were. As the steps went upwards, they became more and more translucent, until near the top of the Altar, or Dias, they were so translucent that the tremendous surging Light beyond, shone through them. I did not dare to go any nearer than the bottom step until invited to do so, but watched in fascination.

At the top of the steps was a curved arch made of white crystal which, like the smaller steps leading up to it, was translucent but it was not that upon which I concentrated so much as the tremendous surging Light beyond. Without the visor, I would not have been able to stand that emanation for a second, and I knew it; without the protective suit, I would have been burnt to a crisp, not by the heat but by the vibrations which emanated from this massive, surging Light — flickering like some strange, cold fire, yet burning in an all-consuming way — and yet not that, because it did not seem to consume, but rather to be built up from Itself. It was as though there was an atomic cycle going on here, as you

THE LOGOS OF EARTH

An impression of the advanced Life Form of the Planet Earth, as seen by the author. This is one of the many transmutations which She demonstrated while in deep mystical communication with other Logoi throughout the Universe.

would imagine the atomic cycle on a miniature Sun. The molecules split to atoms; the atoms were rearranged in some mysterious way unknown to science, to form other atoms which grew in clusters into molecules to be broken down again. As though an inner procreation was taking place from itself, or so it seemed to me. As a matter of fact, the more I gazed intently into this tremendous, living, mystic Flame, the more I seemed to understand Her.

I stood there transfixed — paralyzed — absolutely fascinated by the indescribable movement within this living Flame.

Even as I gazed in fascinated awe at the stupendous power within this Flame, She seemed to change before my very eyes and, for a fraction of a second, She would take on a definite shape, like a large ovoid or part of an ovoid, and then a circle, and then millions of squares, oblongs, pyramids, hexagons, and then these would disappear and the Flame Itself would revert back to giant multicoloured fingers of mystic fire reaching upwards.

I could view this through the large arch which must have been — and this only a guess — at least 150 to 200 feet wide and 200 or 300 feet tall.

I was gazing at the Life Form of a Cosmic Being, so advanced as to become The Logos of a Planet...!

The thought was staggering.

The sight was so magnificent as to be terrifying!

How many men before me have been awed by this experience — I do not know, but I do know that I was thrilled to my very soul.

Seldom have I lived as I lived then.

Typical of yours truly, whose life has been devoted to helping mankind, my thoughts drifted to the ignorance and turmoil on the surface, and then to the fact that here was a part — The Lords had told me but a small part — of the Life Force of this Planet — Earth; a Life Force Who had colossal powers at Her disposal which She could use at any time, but did not do so because to do so would have been to destroy the millions of humanoids crawling over the surface of Her massive, breathing, beautiful body.

I wanted to weep — and I did so.

I have seen kind deeds and heard of kinder deeds, but never a deed as compassionate as this. Here She was, confined to Her self-imposed prison of limitation so that you and I and billions more of us could work our way through our present experience cycle. All She had to do was to use Her stupendous inner powers and few of us would be able to exist on or around this Planet; but those few would not be obsessed, like the majority, by greed and hate and jealousy which, when expressed, results in war and murder and pillage, and untold damage to Her beautiful body.

No, I am not unduly hard on mankind; I have done more for him than most people have ever dreamed about, but I am truthful about the numerous failings of the human race.

What I was seeing was the result of the amalgamation of the Spirits and Intelligences of majestic Beings Who had passed through millions of years of Evolution and deep Cosmic Initiations, even in other parts of the Solar System and Galaxy, before They had earned the right to amalgamate together and become the Life Form of a Planet. This information had been given to the world in 1961 by the great Cosmic Master, Mars Sector 6, Who had, through compassion and feeling for mankind, revealed the greatest secrets of Evolution which have yet been divulged in man's history. Having had the supreme honour to take those Nine Cosmic Transmissions, called, *The Nine Freedoms*, and having written a book on them, I could better appreciate the majestic Form upon which my fascinated gaze was riveted. (Note 11.)

I had heard about Her before from high Cosmic Sources.

I had written about Her.

But now I was actually seeing Her in living, breathing action.

Despite the stupendous movement in those living, cycling Flames, I knew that She must be in a state of quiescence for, had Her full powers been released, even for one second, the energy discharge would have transmuted the massive body of the Planet and She would be able to travel through the skies to whatever destination She so chose, instead of remaining here in supreme sacrifice for the sake of many far less-evolved entities than Herself. I remember blurting through my tears and emotion:

"Why, oh why, in God's Name, does She do it?"

The answer came, calm, gentle, like a cool breeze across a summer desert.

"In your own way, why do you do it — and others before you, why did they do it?"

A question, but so surely a complete answer to my emotional outburst.

I will tell you this, every person on Earth should thank the Divinity in which they believe for creating a Being such as this. A Being Who, because of Her long-suffering compassion, has given you a beautiful classroom on which to gain your experience, on which to evolve towards that Perfect God from Which all things originated.

So absorbed and fascinated had I become with the indescribable movement within that part of The Flame Of The Logos Of Terra, that I was unaware of the crashing sounds around me. It was only when I concentrated on them that I heard the tumultuous rise of this thunderous, all-embracing sound. At one time it would sound like some strange celestial choir at a great distance with indistinguishable words, and at the next time, like some mighty roaring ocean, as though unleashed and uncontrolled. But this was not unleashed or uncontrolled, and this is what made me even more awe-struck at the stupendous power and might and control exercised over it all.

As I gaped in fascinated awe, I realized that just as the influences generated within these ever-moving, ever-changing, flickering patterns of Cosmic Fire were travelling billions of light-years through Space to affect and change other life streams on billions of other inhabited worlds, as indeed was She, The Mighty Logos, contacting, absorbing, learning from other Logoi influences within the Universe. Here was the personification of a vital exchange of influence passing between mighty Body and mighty Body through the firmament of God's Holy Creation.

I felt a cold shudder rack my body as this realization came to me.

Here was indeed an aspect of Cosmic Creation and Cosmic Communication and Cosmic Interchange, so perfectly attuned to each other as only The Divine could create it. And to realize that out there, throughout Space, there were hundreds of millions of Logoi, probably somewhat similar to the One upon Which I gazed, together forming a pattern of The Creator's stupendous Handiwork.

For one glorious moment I wanted to tear the suit from my body, leap up those steps and throw myself headlong into that giant Flame, to be consumed by Her and lost to man forever...!

But I had a Mission to finish.

I do not know whether it was because of an outside prompting from The Lords, or on my own volition, that I turned away and walked towards Them, but for whatever reason, I did so. If it was from my own volition then it probably was because I had seen far more than I deserved to see.

I had lived through one of the greatest experiences possible to any man or Master on Earth and I did not deserve to enjoy that experience for any longer.

Maybe I will never know why I turned away — but with reluctance, did so.

I came back to The Lords and we were all silent for a time.

We passed back through the place where the screen was located and They closed it behind Them and the sound was cut out and gave way to stillness.

After that, The Three Tall, Gracious Beings turned and I followed Them as They walked, apparently quite slowly, across the floor of this massive underground Temple. I knew that it was not detachment on Their part which caused Them to turn abruptly so that I could follow, but compassion. My mind was a receiving centre for thoughts which seemed to race through it at tremendous velocities. But foremost was the vivid picture of those magnificent, moving, mystical Cosmic Flames which reached upwards — forever upwards, depicting the very Heart, the very Life Form Itself of The Great Being on Whom we all lived. I realized that, to my dying day — and well beyond that — I would never forget the experience which I had been most honoured to have been given. I could now better appreciate what The Lords had told me, that no man, in my position, had ever seen the full expression of a Planetary Logos and had lived.

What portion I had seen of Her I do not know, but it was enough to impress me forever and ever and ever....

I will, as the months go past, learn more and more from this Initiation, for an experience as elevated as this one, cannot be translated into language soon after it happens but seems to set a thought pattern in the mind which has the capability of educating itself from itself as though directed by those initial thought impulses. At the time, just after seeing an aspect of The Great Logos, I must say that my mind was numb and it is only afterwards that I really appreciated the experience which I had lived through and the deep Wisdom which this is continually giving to me — even now.

As I slowly followed The Three Majestic Protectors Of The Ineffable Flame Of The Logos Of Terra across that massive underground cavern, I desperately wanted to express some thoughts of thankfulness to Them, but what could I say that They did not already know? It is when this thought entered my mind and I wrestled with it that The Three of Them stopped in front of me and into my mind came another thought from outside, gentle yet definite; not commanding but requesting, in such a manner as, at the time, it was as though I had formulated this thought for myself, but now I feel sure that I did not do so — that the thought was given as guidance to me.

"Say not anything to Us — but to God."

Immediately this realization dawned The Lords stopped and I behind Them. The Taller One looked off into the distance, illuminated by the thousands of globes high above our heads which, as before, had obediently followed our progress. The other Two disappeared, seemed to blink out of existence before my eyes.

I followed His gaze and froze.

After tearing the helmet from my head, I heard the sound as the plastic helmet bounced on the rocky floor at my feet. For there, in front of my staring eyes, a huge and majestic form was slowly but surely starting to build. First walls appeared and then spires atop those walls, stretching hundreds of feet up into the space above our heads. There before my almost unbelieving eyes a Temple was built up!

This structure was made of what appeared to be crystal which shone with an inner light of its own and was so bright that I could see the top of the highest spire, which must have stretched hundreds of feet into the black darkness above me. It was not a simple building; in fact, so complex were the arches and domes and what appeared to be, but were not, carvings on these arches and domes, that I cannot possibly do them even half justice by my simple description. It was like a large cathedral, but not one seen in the western part of the world, rather, if you can imagine, a translucent, glowing, crystalline structure which, from an architectural point of view, was more eastern than a mosque and yet had certain Gothic characteristics about it. I am not an architect, unfortunately, for I could then do more justice to this description.

The body of this Temple was a massive circular globe, with steps leading up to a high arched entrance and around this globe, there were spires towering upwards. On the four sides of the main spheroid structure were large obelisks which, unlike the rest of the rounded spires and domes, were starkly angular. I felt then that these columns were aligned to the exact points of the compass; that may or may not be correct, but it seemed to be so. These obelisks seemed to enhance the Shape Power aspect of the great, shining Temple itself.

On Earth, this would have taken years to build, but I had seen it form before my very eyes in minutes! It was not a trick of illumination either — by that I mean that it was not there previously in darkness and had suddenly been illuminated — I saw it actually **build up** before my staring eyes by miraculous means.

''My God,'' I gasped.

''And Mine,'' came the gentle, reminding telepathic thought from The Lord Who stood and watched me intently.

After this indescribably beautiful Temple, shining with a mystical inner light, which had been instantly built deep in the underground caverns of Earth before my astonished eyes, had been finished, the other Two Lords appeared by the side of The Tall One, Who, rightly or wrongly, I took to be the Spiritual Leader.

There was silence, deep, all-pervading.

A silence which I ''listened'' to with deep concentration.

As though guided by some power superior to my conscious mind, I made my way slowly, in great reverence, towards the steps leading to the open door of this Temple and, without hesitation, started to climb these steps. Although I did not count them then I knew that there were 33 of them. I walked through the open door into the Temple and stood at the back of the Temple, just inside the door.

The inside of the Temple was devoid of any seating, just a large empty space except for the Altar down at the far end of the giant globe in which I stood. It was then that another realization came to me. Many years ago, The Aetherius Society had been instructed to build a Shape Power Temple upon the surface of Earth and I had designed one such Temple which I felt strongly would have tremendous natural powers inherent within it. Although the Temple in which I now stood was in all ways more glorious and complex than my original design, both on the outside and the inside, however, the basic concepts were somewhat similar. (Note 12.)

There is but one obvious move to make when entering any Temple, never mind such a one as this — after any experience, never mind such a one as the experience I had just lived through; that is to thank God for the privilege of being.

I put my hands out in front of myself, the fingers now ungloved, for I had torn the gloves from my hands before I entered, and formed the fingers into the most advanced Mudra which I knew. And then said a Prayer of thankfulness to God for the compassion shown to me and the enlightenment which I had received. Although I was in a projected form, I felt even a further division take place. It was as though I stood even higher, above the projected form itself, inspiring it, for a part of my consciousness, still remaining in the projected form, heard words, the like of which I could not even form. The Prayer started off simply in English and then went into another language of which I was familiar but can only use and understand when in a high state of inspiration. As though this were not enough, I was moved into a different category of language entirely and after a moment of intoning this other strange melodious language, lapsed into silence for I could no longer consciously reduce my Prayers to sound expressions. The great mystical fire of Kundalini manifested in Brahma Chakra and I went into a highly elevated state of mystical experience. I will not report exactly what happened while I was in this elevated state of Cosmic Consciousness although I remember it most vividly. As my motive for coming into this

Temple was to thank God, I detached from the state of Cosmic Consciousness and continued my Prayer of thankfulness. (Note 13.)

I said a Prayer of thanks to God.

This was followed by another heartfelt Prayer of thankfulness to The Logos Of The Planet Earth.

Then a Prayer of thankfulness to The Great Lords Themselves, The Protectors Of The Ineffable Flame Of The Planet Earth.

Lastly, to The Adepts Who had helped and equipped me for my journey to this most Holy Shrine of all Holy Shrines.

After doing this I felt, rather than heard, a prompting urging me to return.

Reluctantly I left this majestic Temple.

While leaving, I counted the steps as I descended and indeed was right, there were 33 steps. There are 33 steps to enlightenment as well, so it was not by chance that The Lords had fashioned 33 steps from the floor of the huge cavern to the entrance of this magnificent Temple.

I realized then, quite acutely, that I had been away from my physical structure for a long time and felt that The Lords were gently urging me to make my return to the surface. I walked back to where the Three of Them stood and knew that it was not necessary for me to say anything because They knew my innermost thoughts of sheer gratitude and must have realized that I could not even begin to do justice to the expression of the depth of feelings of love I held for Them.

I looked down at the floor and saw an alien round shape lying there with a hole in one side of it and bent down and picked it up. It was the helmet I had dropped. I remembered then that I had dropped my gloves before entering the Temple but I did not have to go back and retrieve them for, with a kind, understanding smile, One of The Great Lords handed them to me.

They turned and I followed behind in silence.

How long we walked I do not know as my mind was clear but completely engaged upon the important happenings which had taken place. We must have covered some distance before suddenly, out of the dark abyss above, a green beam of light appeared and The Three Lords stopped on the edge of the perfectly circular reflection made on the crystal floor by the pale green light.

I knew that this was my way back to the surface. I slowly pulled on my gloves, then, after adjusting the dark-coloured visor inside the helmet so that it would not obstruct my vision, I put the helmet on — gave it one quarter turn and sealed it into place.

Just for a moment I hesitated before stepping into the circle and regarded these Three most ancient, most Holy, most wonderful Beings.

I did not know how to express myself.

I realized that They knew that my heart and soul were filled with the wondrous majesty of it all and I felt words were inadequate to express my deep appreciation. I faced the eyes of Each of Them in turn, then looked back into the distance for one last glance at that majestic Temple and even further back towards The Flame Of The Logos.

The Temple was gone.

The Great Lords had put the energies back into the Universal Supply from which They had built it.

I think that far, far, far in the distance I saw a pinprick of brilliant flickering Light, burning like a Star on the horizon of a velvet black night sky.

Reluctantly I stepped into the circle of green light and soon appeared in the cabin of the Spacecraft again.

I felt willing hands take the helmet from my head and the suit from my body. I looked at The Master Babaji and the other Two Adepts and could tell from the expression on Their faces that They, too, had lived through a similar experience at an earlier time. No conversation passed between us for I know that They realized that I did not want to talk about it then. The Master Babaji walked over to me and placed His Holy hand upon my head and I lost consciousness of my surroundings to be shortly aware of other, more mundane, very worldly surroundings in my bedroom in Santa Barbara.

I came back to my terrestrial physical body and when I had gathered my wits sufficiently, half turned over and pressed the metallic button on the black plastic handle of the buzzer. Immediately, my wife came into the room and I asked her what time it was. It was 3:30 p.m.

I had been out of the body for one hour and forty-five minutes.

I should have felt very weak, cold and trembly, but did not feel like this. In fact, it was amazing how well I did feel. It was as though I had only been in deep trance for 10 or 15 minutes and not well into the danger zone — for the danger factor rises abruptly during the state of conscious projection after the first 50 minutes! I did, however, request the oxygen equipment to be brought nearer so that I could strap on the mouth and nose piece. I breathed the oxygen while the others gave Spiritual Healing and massage to my cramped limbs. Soon after that I was able to arise and had no re-percussions from the dangerous projection condition until several hours later. Undoubtedly, the draught which The Lords had, in Their deep compassion, given to me made the wear and tear on the physical and nervous structure of my aging body far less strenuous than it would have been had They not seen fit to administer this. In fact, instead of needing days of recuperation to recover from the dangerously long, deep trance condition, the next morning, on January 24th, I began to start the writing of the last Chapter of this book. It should be remembered that, although the experience which I relate to you here was one that will live in my cherished memory forever, the actual journey to The Protectors Of The Flame and back was a very complicated one, to say the least. The internal nervous trauma caused by the complexity of the journey and the greatness of the experience itself, as well as the absence from my physical structure of one hour and forty-five minutes, should have affected my health for weeks afterwards. But it did not seem to have any detrimental effect; in fact, if anything, just the opposite. Whatever was contained in the draught which The Lords Of The Flame gave to me, certainly helped me in many ways.

And thus ended a great and inspiring experience.

An experience I will never ever forget.

One which, when recalled even in part, still continues to inspire me in the most uplifting manner and I feel that recall of this won-derful meeting with The Protectors Of The Ineffable Flame Of The Logos Of Earth, and the sight of a part of The Mighty God-dess Herself, will continue to inspire, educate and lead me on-wards towards greater accomplishments.

Indeed does God work in mysterious ways His Wonders to perform.

I did not realize when I was given the instructions from the Cosmic Master Aetherius many years ago to devise equipment for a "Power Stabilization Station," that such a complex set of different moves would be put into motion. The more I look back at it all now, the more sure I am that, not only was I guided by the Higher Forces, but also **allowed** this guidance to manifest through me as definite action, on behalf of the human race on this Planet.

Although the occult history given in Chapter 1 of this book is very brief, if you study it carefully it contains sufficient information to prove to all perceptive students that a brilliantly conceived Plan was slowly but surely being worked out. My ideas and inspiration, brought together to devise the mighty "Operation Sunbeam," not only helped mankind, but more important still, inspired other races in this Galaxy to follow suit with their definitions of the same Mission. And gradually, through "Operation Sunbeam," several previous Cosmic Missions were brought together so that these, too, were helped to work out to a much fuller extent than they would have done if "Operation Sunbeam" had not been devised and carried out in a practical manner. Even though I was able to start the "Power Stabilization Station" years before we ever expected to start this in a Mission called "Operation Earth Light," I still did not expect the unique honour which The Protectors Of The Flame saw fit to bestow upon me on that memorable day of the 23rd of January. It seems as though this elevated experience was a highlight in my life which I have shared with you so that it will act as a signpost to show the future road in such a clear manner that none of us should miss it.

I learned many things during that great mystical Initiation while standing transfixed before the cold, mystical Fire which formed an essential part of the Life-Power of The Mighty Logos Of This Planet. But one lesson which I will never forget was, strangely enough, one which I have always known ever since I was a very small child, but this Truth was brought home to me more forcibly than ever before. It is a simple Truth and an obvious one, but has been overlooked by mankind for centuries. It is a Truth which the more highly evolved Beings, living on other Planets in this Solar System, have known about for thousands of years.

Very simply stated, the Truth is this: **The most Holy, the most Sacred, the most God-like Being you have ever physically touched, is the ground beneath your feet.**

If mankind were to appreciate this one very obvious aspect of occult Truth, then with this realization would come a marked change for the better in all of his thought and action, and the history of man's tomorrows would be very different from what it is liable to be if this change is not brought about. Although we are all aspects of the One Divine Creative Principle, however, the Planet Earth upon Whom we live, is millions of lives nearer to God than we who inhabit Her Great Form.

It is indeed the Holiest, most Sacred Aspect of God ever touched by man and should always be regarded and revered as such.

It is not by chance that an ancient Cosmic Being, Who goes under the name of The Master Aetherius, has stated that ''Operation Sunbeam'' is the most important Mission performed by any terrestrials in the world today; that this one Mission alone is more important than all the Spiritual work performed by any country upon the Earth. He said this because He knows, beyond any doubt, that any Spiritual or religious undertaking which is specially devised to help to pay back the debt to The Goddess Terra, owed by all of us, takes precedence in importance over the other actions of mankind. Why? Because of the fact that She is the Holiest Aspect of God which man has yet come into physical contact with.

When ''Operation Earth Light'' is put into action, as it definitely will be, and through this Mission, a small band of terrestrials living on the physical Realms do offer their help directly to The Goddess Herself, this, too, will become another one of the great Missions of the world. This must be so because we are directly helping The Holy One in a very potent manner.

Nothing happens by chance but by design in one way or another. As you give so shall you receive. By Karmic Law, I could not have received the elevated Initiation in the Holiest Temple on Earth unless I had deserved it. Even so, I feel that there was another motive connected to this. It was by design, and not by chance, that The Protectors Of The Flame gave me permission to describe this Initiation to mankind. I can see now very clearly why this was allowed — so that those who were ready would be inspired to become more active Spiritual workers by the message contained in these writings.

The future seems uncertain except in one definite way. Mankind will not be allowed to destroy the Planet Earth by his atomic bungling. Before this happens, he will be stopped, by force if necessary, by the Higher Powers. He can war and kill and maim his brothers if he is callous enough to do so, but he will not be allowed to destroy the body of this Earth as he did the previous Planet upon which he lived. (Note 14.)

Despite the uncertainties of the future, with thermonuclear bombs a constant threat to man's existence, the New Age will come to this Planet to those who are ready. Those who are not ready for this change will be born again on another Planet in this Solar System, which is younger than this Earth and as primitive, from a purely surface point of view, as She was millions of years ago. And then man will have to work his way back though his respective lives so that he may learn to worship — love — and work for God. Those who, by Karmic Law, manipulated by their own correct thought and action, have deserved to inherit the bright New Age, will do so upon this beautiful green Planet — Earth.

I have known these Truths for years. The Initiation I received while in the Holy Presence of The Great Lords and while before The Logos Herself, has reinforced this knowledge.

If you would be wise, then start an investment today by putting good, unselfish deeds into a Spiritual bank account which will pay the highest dividends of all. And let some of those deeds be performed directly for the benefit of the Earth as a Holy Entity — note that, as a Holy Entity, not just a source of physical sustenance. And I know from my own experience that when you do this you will be guided and given the strength and knowledge to succeed and evolve.

The Earth upon Whom you live is a most Sacred and Holy Being — always treat Her as such — always work for Her as such — always Bless Her as such.

GO WITH GOD.

AUTHOR'S RECOMMENDATIONS

NOTE 1. For further information about "Operation Bluewater," study *The Aetherius Society Newsletter*, Volume 2, Issue 5, March; Issues 12 & 13, July-August; Issues 14-16, September 1963; Volume 3, Issues 9 & 10, May; Issues 23 & 24, December 1964; Volume 4, Issues 1 & 2, January; Issues 3-6, February-March 1965. Also study the booklet, *This Is The Hour Of Truth*.

NOTE 2. Read *The Aetherius Society Newsletter*, Volume 19, Issues 1-4, January-February 1980, "Amazing Facts About 1979."

NOTE 3. In July 1978, a vitally important mental communication was received by Doctor George King, for the first time, from a Cosmic Master known as Mars Sector 8 — Special Advisor S2, supplying information enabling far greater precision in the calculation of Spiritual Energy within "Operation Prayer Power" batteries. See *The Aetherius Society Newsletter*, Volume 17, Issue 19, August 1978.

Since that time, this Master has taken a keen interest in The Aetherius Society and has provided information, using computers technologically vastly superior to anything on Earth, greatly in advance of the knowledge which mankind could obtain from any other source.

NOTE 4. 25 Phases of "Operation Sunbeam" were performed in 1979. Four Phases, prior to the improved modus operandi, amounted to 6,000 Prayer Hours of Spiritual Energy, while the subsequent 21 Phases, employing the enhanced modus operandi, doubled the Spiritual Energy output of each Phase and amounted to a further 63,000 Prayer Hours equivalent released to The Logos Of Earth. See *The Aetherius Society Newsletter*, Volume 18, Issues 19-22, October; Issues 29-32, November-December 1979.

For an up-date on this on-going Mission, read *The Aetherius Society Newsletter*, Volume 19, Issues 11-14, June-July 1980; and Journal *Cosmic Voice*, Volume 1, Issues 1-4, August-September 1980; Volume 2, Issues 7-8, May 1981; Volume 3, Issues 8-10, September-October 1982; and Volume 4, Issues 9-12, July-September 1983.

NOTE 5. Due to the contact between Doctor George King and The Cosmic Masters, mankind has been informed since 1955 of the operation of a giant Spacecraft, called Satellite No. 3, which orbits Earth for various periods each year known as Magnetization Periods, or Spiritual Pushes. During these times, Spiritual Energies are radiated from Satellite No. 3 to individuals and groups on Earth who are performing unselfish Service, which results in the enhancement of all Spiritual action by a factor of 3,000 times. For further information on Satellite No. 3, study Chapter 4 of *The Nine Freedoms.* See also *The Day The Gods Came.*

During each Spiritual Push, Spiritual Energies are also radiated by Satellite No. 3 to the world through the two Spiritual Energy Radiators of The Aetherius Society for a minimum of six hours a day. For a greater understanding of this Operation, "Operation Space Power," and for an in-depth study of the immense benefits of the operation of Satellite No. 3 to all Levels of life on Earth, read the book, *Operation Sunbeam — God's Magic In Action.*

NOTE 6. See *The Aetherius Society Spiritual Healing Bulletin* for reports about Spiritual Healing and the tremendous success achieved throughout the world by The Aetherius Society Healing Band.

NOTE 7. See *The Aetherius Society Newsletter,* Volume 12, Issues 8-9, May; Issues 14-17, August 1973; Volume 13, Issues 16-20, August-September; Issues 25-26, December 1974; Volume 14, Issue 18, September 1975; Volume 17, Issues 5-8, March-April; Issue 19, August 1978; Volume 18, Issues 23-24, October 1979; Issues 25-26, October 1979; *Cosmic Voice,* Volume 1, Issues 5-8, October-November 1980; Volume 2, Issues 10-12, August-September 1981; Volume 3, Issues 11-12, November-December 1982; Volume 4, Issues 1-4, January-March 1983; and Volume 5, Issues 5-9, May-July 1984.

NOTE 8. For a full exciting description of the Initiation given to Doctor George King by The Lord Buddha, now Controller of Shamballa, see *The Aetherius Society Newsletter,* Volume 18, Issue 1, January-February 1979.

NOTE 9. For further information regarding the operation of Satellite No. 3, see *The Day The Gods Came*, and Chapter 4 of *The Nine Freedoms*. Also read *The Aetherius Society Newsletter*, Volume 10, Issues 5 & 6, March; Issues 19 & 20, October 1971.

NOTE 10. For a brilliant description of the massive Temple referred to on Level Four by the Cosmic Master Aetherius, listen to Metacassette® No. MC-21, *The Inauguration Of Operation Prayer Power On Level Four*.

NOTE 11. *The Nine Freedoms* is a very advanced treatise on the preparation and evolution of man and should be studied very deeply by all metaphysical students.

NOTE 12. For an artist's impression of a Shape Power Temple designed by Doctor George King, see the pamphlet, *A Temple With Shape Power*.

NOTE 13. For one of the best descriptions available on Cosmic Consciousness, read Chapter 5 of *The Nine Freedoms*, for both the Cosmic Transmission and the author's actual experience of Cosmic Consciousness.

NOTE 14. For further information regarding the Planet Maldek, read the Introduction to *The Nine Freedoms*.

All the cassettes, books and Newsletters recommended above are currently available from the publishers, The Aetherius Society.

EPILOGUE

As reported in Chapter 2 of this book, the Mission "Operation Earth Light," was given the sanction of The Protectors Of The Flame on November 29th, 1979 (Earthyear 16.145). I was informed by my own Holy, revered Master, and later by The Protectors Of The Flame Themselves, that the way we intended to perform "Operation Earth Light" would set a pattern for others to follow. I also stated that, from an occult point of view, it was necessary to make a start on this Mission in 1979, despite the fact that, had I waited before doing so, a start could have been made on a more favourable date which would have changed the astrological implications of the birthday of the Mission. However, I was in possession of information which I was not in a position to reveal at that time. I knew that The Master Babaji, together with other Ascended Masters from The Spiritual Hierarchy Of Earth, were preparing for a Spiritual Pilgrimage throughout the Higher Planes of this Earth. I felt sure that, if official acceptance of "Operation Earth Light" was given by The Lords Of The Flame and because our performance of this Mission was classed as a pattern for others to follow, The Lord Babaji would include the performance of this Mission as an important aspect of His Pilgrimage.

This is exactly what happened.

Shortly after the official acceptance which, of course, The Master Babaji knew about, having made the initial arrangements for the interview with The Protectors Of The Flame, He did set off on His Mystical Pilgrimage throughout the Higher Planes. This Pilgrimage was to be the start of a concerted Spiritual Renaissance which is so necessary in these troubled times. The Karmic pattern of those who inhabit the Higher Realms was ready for such a Renaissance and The Master Babaji took advantage of this.

The Pilgrimage was started in December, 1979 (Earthyear 16), on what is termed as Level Two, and from there proceeded up to the Higher Levels, taking each one in turn and ending on the Highest inhabited Realm connected to this Planet, namely, Level Six. During this time The Master Babaji, because of His highly elevated station, drew enormous crowds of eager students to all meetings on these Realms, especially those including Level Three and above.

During this Pilgrimage, The Lord Babaji and His retinue of chosen Ascended Masters stressed the tremendous importance of the Earth as an Entity and the fact that She should be regarded more as a Holy Being than She had been in the past. He also stressed the fact, as I knew He would, that Missions such as ''Operation Sunbeam'' and ''Operation Earth Light'' were vitally important to the Karmic pattern of mankind on all Levels of existence. The Master Babaji, together with Adepts ''Nixies Zero Zero Four'' and ''Nixies Zero Zero Five,'' actually interviewed scientists on the Higher Realms who were willing and able to start and promote ''Operation Earth Light'' on those Realms.

The Spiritual Hierarchy Of Earth have already started ''Operation Sunbeam'' on the physical Realm and, without going into detail at this stage, I can say briefly that certain receptive Psychic Centres in the body of Earth, which The Aetherius Society, because of lack of funds, is unable to deal with, will be Charged by The Great White Brotherhood. For a number of complex reasons, no way has yet been devised to promote ''Operation Sunbeam'' on anything but the physical Realms of this Planet. The Adepts have been working for many years, together with the finest scientific brains from the Higher Realms, to design and use certain extremely sophisticated equipment which will make it possible for the Higher Realms to cooperate in ''Operation Sunbeam,'' but as this book is being written, this equipment has just been put into operation. Hence the wisdom of The Lord Babaji in not pushing for Higher Realm cooperation in ''Operation Sunbeam'' at this time but concentrating on ''Operation Earth Light'' as this is a Mission in which all Realms can and must cooperate.

I would like to offer my thanks and Blessings to The Master Babaji and to both of The Adepts Who took valuable time away from Their Spiritual Pilgrimage to provide me with transport during my last visit to The Holy Protectors Of The Flame.

The reports I have received from The Spiritual Hierarchy Of Earth up to this time are most gratifying, to say the least. Thousands of people have come forward to help in the promotion of

"Operation Earth Light" and have volunteered to help to set up "Power Stabilization Stations" in different parts of the Higher Realms on which they live. For security reasons, because the greatest good in the wrong hands can become the most dangerous, these volunteers will be carefully screened so that we can guarantee that no interfering forces can learn the secrets of our apparatus.

If you study with care the supplementary reading matter recommended by the author in this book, you will see that, under certain conditions, it is possible for powerful forces from the lower astral Realms to project onto the Higher Realms for a short time, and this enables them to learn many important secrets unless a strict security control is kept. This is one reason why security is absolutely essential. However, it can be stated now that, in the near future, thousands of intelligences who, because of their Spiritual advancement on Earth and who now inhabit the Higher Realms, will be cooperating in "Operation Earth Light." As far as the physical Realms are concerned, The Aetherius Society is working towards setting up a "Power Stabilization Station" and, in the near future, we should have this fully active.

It seems that once again an idea inspired by The Cosmic Masters and put into activation by a devoted team of terrestrials has spread throughout the Intelligentsia of a Planet.

"Operation Sunbeam" spread like beams of thought-light throughout the Galaxy.

"Operation Earth Light" has not done this yet, but has spread throughout the Planet Earth, and who knows, may be adopted by other outside worlds if such an adoption is necessary.

As previously stated, as far as our activation of "Operation Earth Light" is concerned, the Spiritual Energy released by The Goddess Terra through our equipment will be transmitted to the Devic Kingdom and thereby give the Devas pure, unconditioned, uncoloured energy with which to work. This will have an indirect effect upon mankind for the better.

Thus, more than ever before in our previous history, is a deeper appreciation of the vast importance and Holiness of The Goddess Terra being realized in an active way, not only by a few living on the physical Realms, but by thousands of more advanced people now on the Higher Realms.

That "Operation Earth Light" will turn out to be one of the most important ecological tools of all time there is no doubt.

When you have sanction from Masters of the undoubted calibre of The Lord Babaji, Spiritual Head Of The Spiritual Hierarchy Of Earth, and His Ascended Masters, together with the brilliant Adepts, immediately recognizing the importance of "Operation Earth Light," then there can be no doubt whatsoever, in any logical thinker's mind, that the performance of this Mission is of such importance as to overrule most other things. Neither can there be any doubt in any deep thinker's mind that any Mission which is either designed to assist The Goddess Terra, as is "Operation Earth Light," or any Mission designed to pay back a token of the immense debt owed by mankind to The Goddess Terra, as is "Operation Sunbeam," that such actions are so vastly important that they tend to make other Spiritual actions tiny in comparison. It is because both of these Missions are specifically designed to directly help The Goddess Herself, as an Entity, which gives them an importance above other things. It is because The Goddess Terra is so Holy, so advanced, that anything designed to assist One such as Her must take a priority in importance over all other things.

When you realize this in your thoughts and actions, your future will be a sure journey into God-appreciation and broad enlightenment. The vast individual and collective Karmic improvements which will be brought about by the true recognition of The Goddess Terra, and actions to pay back the debt which all men owe to this Goddess, will be such that, at some future time, you will have a chance to live through the type of experience which was enjoyed by the author of this book.